What's a Mom to Do!

JULIE HAGSTROM
author of *Games Babies Play*

Produced by The Miller Press

A FIRESIDE BOOK
Published by Simon & Schuster, Inc.
NEW YORK

Copyright © 1985 by The Miller Press, Inc.

A Fireside Book,
Published by Simon & Schuster, Inc.
Simon & Schuster Building
Rockefeller Center
1230 Avenue of the Americas
New York, New York 10020

FIRESIDE and colophon are registered trademarks of Simon &
Schuster, Inc.

Designed by Stanley S. Drate/Folio Graphics Co., Inc.

Manufactured in the United States of America

10 9 8 7 6 5 4 3 2 1

Library of Congress Cataloging in Publication Data

Hagstrom, Julie
  What's a mom to do.

  "A Fireside book."
  1. Child rearing—Anecdotes, facetiae, satire, etc.
2. Mother and child—Anecdotes, facetiae, satire, etc.
I. Title.
HQ769.H237   1985   649'.1   84-27561
ISBN 0-671-49707-3

This book is for Amy and Katie
because as Babar once said to Queen Celeste,
"Truly it is not easy to bring up a family . . .
but I wouldn't know how to get along
without them anymore."

Acknowledgments

I would like to thank those friends and neighbors who willingly helped out with car-pools and baby-sitting.

A special thanks also goes to my mother and father, who read as I wrote and always remembered where they laughed.

And last but not least, I'd like to thank my husband for being proud of me.

Contents _____ ♦

Introduction

This is a book about advice. And it's a book about my two kids: Amy, now seven, and Katie, four and a half. They are typical kids, growing up in the usual way—spilling milk, cutting teeth, begging for a dog, throwing up in the car, refusing to nap, eating sand, catching cold, and hating vegetables. I'm a typical mother, handling problems in the usual way—scolding and comforting, bribing and threatening, laughing and crying, and perhaps more than anything else, worrying. Worrying whether or not I am doing the right thing. And that's where the advice comes in. Yes, advice can be a tricky thing. You have to look at it from two sides, who's asking and who's giving.

In the following stories, I'm the one asking, and it isn't necessarily because I don't know what to do. In the past seven years, I've been right more often than not, but I don't always have enough confidence in my own judgment. No one does. I mean, being a parent is a terrific responsibility; there's so much at stake! And to make matters worse, it's not always black or white. What's best for one child may not be right for another. There are no easy answers. Here's a quick story about easy answers. Not too long ago, Amy brought home one of Betty McDonald's delightful *Mrs. Piggle-Wiggle* books from her school library. Mrs. Piggle-Wiggle, so the story goes, is a widow living somewhere in a Middle American neighborhood. "Nobody knows how old Mrs. Piggle-Wiggle is. She says she doesn't know herself. She says, 'What difference does it make how old I am when I shall never grow bigger?' . . . Every child in town is a friend of Mrs. Piggle-Wiggle's but she knows few of their parents. She says grown-ups make her nervous." Get the picture? Anyway, it all started because Herbert Prentiss wouldn't pick up his toys, and when his fit-to-be-tied mother called her friend Mrs. Grapple for advice, she told her to call Mrs. Piggle-Wiggle. "I have heard she is perfectly wonderful. All the children in town adore her and she has a cure for everything. As soon as I spank Susan, I am going to call her."

So Mrs. Prentiss called Mrs. Piggle-Wiggle and, sure enough, she knew just what to do. She explained her old-fashioned Won't-Pick-Up-Toys Cure, and Mrs. Prentiss spent the rest of the day humming a happy tune. Indeed, Mrs. Piggle-Wiggle had a cure for everything from Tattle-tailitis to Bad Table Manners. Sometimes a pinch of magic dust placed behind the ear did the trick, other times the solution lay in a dose of Mrs. Piggle-Wiggle's old-fashioned common sense. She passed no judgment on parent or child; she had, after all, heard it all before. She simply offered an efficient, foolproof way to cure any number of childhood complaints, that is, an easy answer. Yes, I decided that Mrs. Piggle-Wiggle's appeal lay in the fact that she removed the doubts. The parents in her stories still had to carry out her instructions, but there was no longer any question of whether or not it was the right thing to do. Confidence was restored and the parents were put back in charge, humming a happy tune. But alas, Mrs. Piggle-Wiggle has an unlisted number and I am afraid we are on our own. But we have each other, right? And this is what my stories are all about.

So now look at those giving the advice. Look it up in a book first, is my theory. If you find the answer there, you'll save yourself the embarrassment of asking your friends stupid questions. There are all kinds of reference books on child raising, some dealing more in psychological development than in physical, some dealing strictly with discipline and behavior, while others take a more general view of the child from birth to age seven or twelve. The table of contents is a good place to start if your concern is of a general nature—what to expect of a toddler in the realm of language and communication, for instance. But if your needs are more specific—say, biting (human and/or animal)—the index may be the place to look. You have to keep in mind that, although books are written and researched by experts, they need to be adapted to fit your particular child's needs. I usually just keep reading until I find a book that agrees with my way of thinking.

After I've exhausted my written resources, I call Maggie. Maggie's a good friend with two girls very close in age to my two, and a boy. We compare notes a lot. It's nice to have someone like that around. But calling Maggie is easier said than done. She's a real phone person. You know, loves to talk on the phone, just plunges right in and fills you in on all the latest developments in her life. It's sometimes difficult to remember why you called, but it's never dull!

And then there's my mother. Really and truly, what would a girl do without her mother? You think you'll grow out of it, that need for her support, guidance, and, yes, approval. But don't kid yourself. I haven't and, to be perfectly honest, I have no intention of doing so; I need her. But that's okay, she needs me too, you know. And only with your mother can you drone on and on about your children's achievements and successes. Actually, that may be more valuable than her listening to all the woes and worries those same children have caused. I mean, there are a lot of people you can complain to, but only to a grandmother can you brag. And I love to brag about my kids because my mother just eats it up. She's wonderful that way, but she's there on the rough days, too. She's just a good person to ask advice from because she likes to keep things simple. She can cut right to the heart of the matter and give you her honest opinion instantly. In fact, you'll get her honest opinion on several subjects. You know how that is, she *is* my mother and feels she has a right to speak up. So when she's on a roll . . . well, you'll see.

My husband, I would guess, is really no different from most. He's hard-working, level-headed, not very mushy, and right about most things. I don't mean he *thinks* he's right (which of course he does), he really *is* right. But then, it's sometimes easier to be right when you can leave such problems as bed-wetting, back talk and nail biting behind each morning. The fast pace of a classroom teacher may be exhausting but it does allow Jerry a perspective that my part-time work doesn't. So when a problem comes up at home, I rely heavily on my husband's clear and logical advice.

So now that you know who's doing the asking and who's giving the advice, let's get down to the business at hand—kids and what to do about them.

1

A Question
of Quiet

Before Amy was born, I'll admit, I was somewhat apprehensive. Never having had any experience with a tiny baby before, I worried I would not know how to take care of him or her. Well, you can imagine my relief when, after giving birth to a healthy baby girl, my anxieties vanished. Once I held that small bundle in my arms and pressed my cheek against hers, I realized that maternal instincts and common sense were all I really needed to get us through those first few weeks. *And I had all kinds of outside help.* Not only were family and friends in abundance, but I had a shelf lined with books on how, when, where, and why kids do what they do from birth through some distant age like five or seven. I was set. I couldn't wait to get home and be the one in charge. You know how it is, you can't spend fifteen minutes figuring out how to get the diaper on in front of those efficient hospital nurses, but at home, with no one looking over your shoulder, you can change a diaper or give a bath any old way you want! Yes, I was ready. Why, just the day before, my mother had called me on the phone to see how I was doing. She had hemmed and hawed about asking if I felt "down" or anything. When I assured her I felt terrific, she seemed quite relieved.

"Oh, well, that's good to hear. You know this is the day you should have postpartum blues."

"Oh, really? Gosh, I didn't realize. Well, I'll work on it, but really, I don't think I'm going to do that. Are you sure it's today?"

"That's what your sister-in-law said. But I'm glad to hear you're not letting it get to you. Such a drag."

"Absolutely, I think I'll just pass on the postpartum blues!"

Oh, I felt smug! And I certainly wasn't going to get bogged down in a lot of emotional trappings. I had the situation under control.

Once home from the hospital I did quite well, maintaining composure even when Caesar (our undersized German shepherd) lunged his front paws onto the crib to see what everyone was looking at and my neighbor warned us that she'd heard of a dog who tipped over a bassinet and mauled the baby sleeping in it. Did I need to hear that story? But, no matter, I was under control.

However, I wanted things quiet when Amy was sleeping. I mean I just didn't want her to wake up before she was ready because then it would be too early to feed her, and even though I could give her some water, she really didn't like it, and rocking her would help for a while, but I was counting on her sleeping at least another hour, and you understand, don't you? So when I ran outside and chased a motorcycle down the street screaming, "Stop driving by my house! I have a new baby!" I didn't feel I was out of line. Well, listen, it was the third time he'd done it, and I swear he revved up his engine right by Amy's window. He explained he was working on the carburetor and needed to drive it after each adjustment. Living at the end of a cul-de-sac, he had no choice but to ride by the house. Well, I'm a reasonable person and certainly don't expect this kid to alter his plans just because I have a new baby, so I suggested that he walk the motorcycle past my house and drive it on the next block. And, of course, if he didn't, I'd call the police. There, now what was wrong with that?

That was on a Tuesday, and by Thursday I had alienated several neighbors whose lawnmowers and filters were making me frantic with their constant droning, which seeped into the house. I had a call in to the air force base asking if they had recently changed their flight pattern—the planes seemed to come so much lower and more often the past few days. They hadn't returned my call, however. By the time my husband came home from work Friday night, I had stopped the pendulum on the grandfather clock ("It's not just the chiming every hour, but did you ever notice how loud it *ticks*?"), taken the phone off the hook, and put masking tape over the doorbell. I remember him saying something about extremes and a morgue, but, hey, *he* wasn't home all day worrying about a baby who might be awakened at an inappropriate time by a sudden noise, or a constant noise, or an irregular noise, or even a quiet noise. Why, he didn't begin to understand the range and variety of noises from which a mother struggles to protect her baby. After all, he had spent his day freely opening and closing doors, scooting in and out of chairs without a second thought, talking in a normal tone of voice and probably even laughing out loud! And me? I'd been tiptoeing around the house and going outside to clear my throat. But I guess that's just how it is with a new baby, right? I think I'm under control.

It must have been that night, as my husband walked through the house switching off lights and locking doors before going to bed, that I crossed the fine line.

"What is all that noise?"

"What noise? I don't hear anything."

"That . . . I don't know, buzzing sound."

"Those are crickets, Julie. Your average crickets-in-the-summer grass crickets. Okay?"

"God, they're loud. Is it mating season or something? There must be a million of them. I'd better close Amy's window."

"Why? It's hot in there."

"But . . . the crickets are so loud tonight. They might wake her." And even as I said it, I knew how it sounded.

"Julie, tell me you're kidding!"

"Well, I just meant . . ."

"Oh, for heaven's sake! Trust me. The crickets won't wake Amy. Now go to sleep."

But I couldn't sleep, not with those crickets making all that racket outside of Amy's open window. I slipped out of bed. Now, going into Amy's room when she was asleep could be tricky. First of all, there was the actual opening of the door. I found that if you slowly squeezed the knob while at the same time lifing up on the door, you'd avoid rattling the door in its frame. Then you slowly turned the knob. At about half way around the latch, there would be a terrific *click,* and your best bet at this point was to freeze, hold your breath, and strain your ears for any sounds of movement from within the room. Should you hear a rustling or, God help you, a whimper, you'd have no choice but to slowly release the doorknob and tiptoe quickly away.

The night of the crickets, however, there was no sound from within, so I slowly opened the door. Now, you could only open the door about a fourth of the way because any further resulted in a terrible creaking noise. So I sidled through the partially opened door and took my four giant steps around the perimeter of the room, pressing my back against the wall. You had to avoid the center of the room at all costs because it groaned and moaned under the slightest weight. So I groped my way along the wall like a cat burglar on a window ledge until I got to the open window. The sound of the crickets was almost deafening! I looked over at Amy's sleeping figure. Oh, really, look at that sweet baby. Her head was turned toward me, and I could just make out her small hand resting alongside her stuffed bear. Might I dare two giant steps across that hazardous floor to get a closer look and perhaps stroke her blanketed back? What the heck, a mother's love knows no bounds. I struck out across the floor and reached her crib safely. Gazing down at her, I was overwhelmed with love and joy and . . .

"Julie? What are you doing?"

I couldn't believe it! He was calling to me! There was no way for me to answer. I tiptoed quickly to the window.

"Where are you?"

Oh, honestly! Caught between him waking her (a sure thing) and the window sliding shut waking her (a probable thing), I chose the window. *Screeetch!* I moved quietly around the edge of the room, squeezed through the parti-ally opened door, and eased it shut behind me. Lucked out! She didn't even stir.

"Don't call to me when I'm in Amy's room. I can't possibly answer you."

"I didn't know you were in her room. What were you doing? You didn't close her window, did you?"

"It was getting cool in there."

Heavy sigh. "I think you're getting weird about this."

I must have drifted off because the next thing I knew I was awakened by the dog, who was scratching at his ear. Such a racket he was making! The tags on his collar jangled together so loudly he sounded like the tambourines in the Salvation Army Marching Band. And, typical, he was lying right next to Amy's door. I got out of bed and removed his collar. There, silence settled around us again, and I glanced at the digital clock by the bed. 12:18. Let's see, she last ate at ten o'clock and should sleep *at least* until two. I sank back against the pillows. Jerry started to get out of bed.

"Where are you going?"

"I have to go to the bathroom."

"Now? I mean, can't you wait until morning?"

"What?"

"Well, it's just that when you flush the toilet, the water rushes through those pipes in Amy's wall and, I don't know, makes so much noise."

"You are sick. You have let this noise thing get to you. Amy is fine! She sleeps great! She's a healthy, normal baby, and you need to lighten up. Now I am going to the bathroom and I don't want to hear any more about it!"

"Just, please, don't flush the toilet," I whispered into the empty room.

As I lay wondering what had become of the cool, confident self of a few days ago, I heard some sort of roar start up in the kitchen. Now what? I slipped out of bed and followed the noise to the refrigerator. The motor had kicked on, resuming its monotonous hum. I got down on my hands and knees and was reaching for the plug when the kitchen light went on and I saw Jerry standing in the doorway.

"Julie, I think we have a problem."

He was right. I was definitely overreacting to the slightest sound, but shouldn't a house be quiet and conducive to sleep? How much adjusting should a baby have to do and how much should a family quiet down for a baby? It was time to call in some outside help.

What the Books Said

Hoping that Dr. Spock could shed some light on this situation, I reached for my crisp new copy of *Baby and Child Care*. I looked up "Noise" in the index, but it went from "Nipples" to "Nose," so I checked the Table of Contents for the infancy section most appropriate for my problem. "Crying in the Early Weeks" and "Can You Spoil a Baby?" were close but not exactly what I needed. I thought I had it, though, when I discovered the "Enjoy Your Baby, Don't Be Afraid of Him"section. While there wasn't any mention of noise, Dr. Spock did say, "Don't be afraid to respond to other desires of his as long as they seem sensible to you and as long as you don't become a slave to him." I think "sensible" and "slave" are our key words here. A little further on I read something interesting. In the chapter "Parental Doubts Are Normal," there was a paragraph about new mothers' feelings of anxiety. "Most women find that they are more anxious than usual the first few weeks at home. It's probably instinctive for mothers to be overly protective at this period. Fortunately it wears off." So, you see! It's perfectly normal. I've just got stronger instincts than most. And the good news is, "it wears off," just like disappointment, excitement, or old nail polish.

Although I was feeling better already, I decided to see what *The First Twelve Months of Life* had to say on the subject. Here I learned that babies are born hearing and that they prefer certain sounds to others, and it even mentioned that "Many mothers report that the hum of motors, music, soft rhythmic drumming and human voices calm fussy, irritable babies." Could that possibly be true?

About to skip the postpartum-blues section I decided to read it over instead. Interestingly enough, a lot of the feelings of confusion and self-doubt mentioned in correlation to the blues were similar to what I had been experiencing. Could it be I hadn't escaped that condition I was so scornful of just last week after all?

What Maggie Said

When I called Maggie, I learned that her sister-in-law had dropped out of law school, her tomatoes were being destroyed by worms, and the couch she had ordered six months ago still wasn't in. Oh, and about noise and the new baby, Maggie said, "Oh, Julie, really, you *have* to get her used to the normal hubbub of the house. Amanda takes her morning nap right out in the living room, such a hassle to go up and down the stairs, you know. The TV's on and people come and go. That's my advice—just be yourself!"

"Well, let me ask you, Maggie, did you *ever* get the postpartum blues?"

"Oh, something terrible!"

"Why didn't you *ever* say anything?"

"I didn't know that that was my problem, for one thing. And I was feeling so inferior to everyone that I was too ashamed to admit it, or ask for help. It's an awful feeling."

"I think that may be part of my problem. I'm just so tense about keeping everything quiet." I didn't go into any detail. The absurdity of my behavior was beginning to dawn on me.

"Well, just recognize it for what it is and don't take it personally—it happens to the best of us. It'll pass."

"Thanks, Maggie, I feel better already."

What My Mother Said

My mother jumped right into this one. "Well, of course it

should be quiet when Amy's sleeping. In the day, close her door, take the phone off the hook, and put a *Baby Sleeping* sign on her door so those neighborhood kids don't come over and ring your bell. Really, Julie, you should speak to their parents, you're *way* too nice to them. It's ridiculous that they need to see the baby every day. Anyway, at night keep the TV turned down and put the dog outside. Actually, you ought to get rid of that animal. I mean he's in the way all the time, and I think he leers at Amy. But that's up to you. Well, that's all I have to say, but really, Julie, unplugging the refrigerator and calling the air force base! You need more rest. I'll come over tomorrow and take care of Amy so you can catch up on your sleep. You know, you probably won't admit it, but I'll bet you've got a touch of the blues."

"I'm okay, really, Mom. Thanks a lot." How is it that they always know?

What My Husband Said

Since I already knew that my husband thought I was slipping away from the rational world, I wasn't sure I wanted to hear what else he had to say.

"Julie, just go about your life in a normal way. You're making everyone, including Amy, nervous. You're a good mother and you're doing a good job, just relax and enjoy yourself." The combination compliment and criticism made me cry.

"Are you all right?" The poor guy looked worried.

"I'll be fine. I guess I'm just overly sensitive these days." Men don't want to know about postpartum blues. It's like menstrual cramps—they'll say they believe you, but they really don't. No, there was no need to discuss hormonal imbalances or feelings of inadequacy with him. He would nod sympathetically, then ask if I had ironed his blue shirt yet. I smiled to myself.

"What's so funny?" he asked.

"You."

He pulled me into his arms for a gentle hug. "Did you get a chance to fix the pocket on my brown pants?"

See, what did I tell you?

What I Did

I followed my mother's advice, except I didn't call the neighbor kids' parents and I didn't get rid of the dog. I did, however, let her come over and take care of Amy so I could rest. And I made a special effort to do as my husband suggested—relax, enjoy myself and my baby, and let my maternal instincts and common sense take over, like I had planned to do from the beginning.

The beginning . . . ah yes, I remember now. What was it I had said? "I'll just pass on the postpartum blues," I believe it was. Well, I'll tell you, parenting can be a humbling experience.

2

The Adjustment of Amy

I'm the middle child in my family. You know, the one who lacks any real self-confidence or identity because of being lost in the shuffle. I lucked out, really. What a frightening prospect to be the firstborn. Who would willingly volunteer for the job of testing out untried parents? Yes, it's a special breed of baby that goes first. Being first bears with it the responsibility of living up to high (we're talking first-woman-president stuff) expectations, but it also has the special aura of being number one and, for a time at least, the only one. So perhaps the toughest part of being the first is adjusting to not being the only. I know this, and when I found myself pregnant for the second time, I set out to make the baby's arrival as easy and painless for Amy as possible. Indeed, concern over Amy's delicate ego occupied more of my time than did what to name the new baby! But then we had been through a lot, Amy and I. We had met the spoon and conquered it. We had endured the pain of cutting new teeth, ear infections, and diaper rash. Together we had mastered sitting up, crawling, and walking. Together we had suffered sleepless nights in the power struggle for control. And together we had gone cold turkey. And when you've shared the pride of lacy underpants in lieu of diapers, there's no bond so close. And now we were faced with a new challenge.

Not to worry, I knew just what to do. First of all, Jerry and I decided not to tell Amy right away. A two-year-old's concept of time is so vague that nine, or even seven, months would be difficult to grasp. So we were very mature and waited all of five weeks before we broke down and shared the glad tidings with her. I don't know what it is about saying, "You're going to be a big sister," but it's really such a thrill, and for some ridiculous reason I felt genuinely proud of Amy at that moment. Her family position had shifted, and Amy had become one of us. We were waiting for the new baby. In the few seconds it took to tell her the news she changed from being the baby in the family to being the big sister, and it never occurred to me that maybe she wasn't ready to give that up.

So we began Amy's baby-awareness program by a visit to the doctor's office, where she was allowed to hear the baby's heartbeat, her own, and mine. This was good, and as soon as we got home she set up her own doctor's office with her dolls. She pressed her toy stethoscope to their chests and listened intently for the *woosh, woosh* of the baby's heart. It didn't worry me, really, that after each examination Amy would hurl the "patient" across the room. These aggressions needed to be worked out.

Fortunately, I had a few friends with new babies and so arranged visits during the long waiting period. Amy was intrigued by these oversized dolls and would have liked to get a rise out of them, except that their overprotective mothers fluttered around, pushing Amy's hands away from the baby's head and explaining that babies don't like loud noises. I secretly felt that these mothers *were* overreacting. Poor Amy, she only wanted to *see* the baby. Before long she would lose interest in the baby, finding its toys much more fascinating, and would spend the rest of the visit squeaking ducks, spinning tops, and winding up musical lambs. On the way home in the car, we would discuss the baby and how the mom was worried that Amy might accidentally scare her.

"I only wanted to feel her," said Amy.

"I know, honey. I don't blame you. I was *dying* to hold her myself, but I guess Janet just didn't want us to," I answered. "But when we have our own baby we can do whatever we want! Right?" I boasted.

"Can I pinch him?"

"Why would you want to pinch him?"

"To see if he'll cry."

Somehow I had lost my enthusiasm for the conversation.

The big day drew closer, and Amy and I busied ourselves fixing up the baby's room. As we painted Amy's old crib, we talked about what new babies are really like.

"You know, little babies don't really do much of anything. They sleep almost all the time," I said casually. Wouldn't it be great if that were true, I thought to myself.

"But he'll want to go into his little swing. And I can crank it up and get him started!" Amy reminded me cheerfully.

"Well, after a while, but not right away. He'll even be too little for that at first." I was trying to prepare her for this blob who would in no way interfere with her life, and she was looking forward to a real live doll she could dress up and carry around! I tried again, "I want you to understand that in the beginning the baby won't be able to play with his toys or do much of anything. But that's okay! You and I will have lots of time to read books and play with your trucks while we're waiting for this dumb baby to grow up!"

"Well, can I use his swing until he's bigger, then?" she asked.

"You're a little big, but we can try it."

So for the rest of the morning Amy sat in the baby swing kicking her legs and saying, "Goo, goo, ga, ga," while I finished painting the crib.

My due date came and went, and still no baby. The anticipation was hard on all of us, but I was confident that we had done a good job in preparing Amy. Hidden in my closet I even had a supply of small gifts to let Amy open if a visitor should arrive with something for the baby. Like I said before, not to worry.

Katie was born a week late. Grandma came and stayed with Amy while Jerry and I went to the hospital, and Amy came visiting the next day. She looked different to me, kind of lost, really. Her hair was sticking up funny in the front, and she had her T-shirt on backward. I felt a sudden tug at my heart for this child.

"Come here and give Mom a big kiss. I've missed you!" I said to her. She came over and climbed up beside me on the bed. When I gave her a hug she clung tightly to my neck. She smelled of pancake syrup. "Did you have pancakes at Grandma's this morning?" I asked. But she didn't answer my question. Instead, she started pulling at the curtain that ran on a track around each bed. "Don't, honey, you'll get it off its track." Again she ignored me. Changing the subject, I said, "Have you seen your little sister yet?"

"Uh-huh, with Grandma."

"What do you think? Pretty little, huh?"

"Yeah, she looked all squished. Are you coming home today?" she asked.

"No, after two more nights I'll be home. Not tomorrow, but the next day," I tried to explain. She began to tug on the curtain again and this time managed to completely close us off from the rest of the room.

"Why can't you come home now?"

"Well, a person has to rest after having a baby! And the doctors need to make sure Katie's okay," I said with false cheerfulness. The significance of the curtain closing around the two of us wasn't lost on me, and I had a sinking feeling the adjustment was going to be harder than I'd anticipated. "Why don't we all walk down and peek in at Katie? C'mon, Amy, I'll show you around."

After our visit to the nursery, Amy and Grandpa went to see what goodies were to be found in the gift shop, and I had a moment alone with my mother.

"Do you think Amy's doing okay?" I asked.

"Oh, sure. She'll adjust. She's just kind of quiet right now . . . it's got to all sink in. Once you're home she'll feel better."

That was good enough for me. For the remainder of my stay I tried not to worry about Amy. She visited regularly, looking forward to the desserts off my meal tray, and brought me colorful drawings to decorate my room.

Finally home from the hospital, I looked forward to settling down to a normal routine and giving Amy the attention she needed. It was a good plan, and once we got rid of the harmonica, things did go more smoothly . . . for a while. I mean, it really wasn't Amy's fault she had a cold. And while I didn't want one-week-old Katie to get sick, I also couldn't bear to be reprimanding Amy constantly for breathing germs or worse into Katie's face. In the end I decided to put Katie's antibodies to the test and let Amy cuddle and snuggle to her heart's content. And maybe I was imagining things in my weakened state of mind, but I was convinced that Amy was overdoing it. Did she *really* need to kiss Katie before and after every nap? Was it *really* necessary for Amy to lie so close to Katie that their noses touched? Nobody's antibodies were *that* strong.

When Amy was an infant, she had loved her baths. She used to stretch out her legs and kick like a frog in the few inches of water it took to fill her rubber tub. She'd laugh and gurgle, and we'd all have a delightful time. Katie's daily baths, on the other hand, amounted to nothing less than a struggle for her survival.

"She always cries in her bath," Amy remarked one day as we made all the necessary arrangements for Katie's bath.

"Well, honey, I think that when you squeezed the washcloth above her head last time, she got water in her eyes," I said simply.

"Oh."

"Today, you'll be in charge of feet. It'll be your job to get all ten toes clean!" I tried to make it sound important, when really I just wanted her where she'd do the least amount of damage. But what I didn't realize was that while a baby's toes may be quite flexible, they really cannot be bent clear back onto the top of the foot. Nor can they be spread wide enough to allow an entire bar of soap to pass between them. When Katie began to cry, Amy said, "See? There she goes crying again."

"Amy, she cries because you are too rough! Now go to your room and let me finish in peace!" I blew up. Well, it had to be said. She *was* too rough, and it wasn't fair to Katie.

When it got to be time to feed Katie I made sure that Amy was completely settled before I started. This could get tricky.

"Amy, I'm going to feed Katie now. Would you like to sit with me and watch *Sesame Street*?" I asked.

"No, I'm busy," she answered.

"What are you doing?"

"Playing trucks."

"Okay." But I turned *Sesame Street* on anyway. I'm no dummy; we'd been through this scenario before. "Would you like some juice?"

"No, thanks." But I set out a can of apple juice anyway. Katie had no sooner started contentedly nursing than Amy appeared in the living room doorway.

"Could I have some juice now?"

"There's a can of apple juice on the dining room table," I answered, feeling *very* smug.

"I wanted orange juice."

You know, she was really beginning to get on my nerves.

"Well, drink the apple juice and I'll get you the orange juice later."

"No, I'll get it myself."

"No, no . . . the pitcher is too full and it's on that top shelf. . . . Wait . . . I'm coming."

Clutching Katie firmly under her back, I made a dash into the kitchen to prevent the disaster of the day. I grabbed the orange juice container just as Amy tipped it precariously out of the refrigerator. After pouring her some juice, I hobbled back into the living room, Katie still clinging on for dear life. Determined not to shout at her again, I said, "Amy, I know you want my attention and that it's hard for you to share me with Katie, but you're going to have to get used to it. Now, why don't you sit here with us and watch TV?"

There was a pause as she gulped down her orange juice. "Okay," she finally answered, "but can I have a box of raisins? I know right where they are. . . ." I closed my eyes and leaned back in the rocking chair, trying hard not to let my frustrations sour Katie's milk. Life was tough enough.

When Jerry came home that evening and asked how things were going, I said, "Amy's driving me nuts. She's so heavy-handed with Katie. She pushes the baby swing so hard Katie practically flies out, a pat on Katie's back is more like a slug, and you should have seen her washing poor Katie's feet. I swear, she is trying to do her in."

"That bad, huh?" he mocked.

"Oh, terrific, laugh at me."

"Oh, Julie, I'm not laughing at you, but it's only natural for her to be jealous. Actually, I think she's handling it all quite well."

"Well, we'll see."

Jerry's brother and his wife came to visit that night along with their ten-year-old twin girls. They all crowded into the living room, where I was holding Katie.

"Oh! She's *so* cute!"

"And look at that lovely skin!"

"And hair! She's got your curls, Julie!"

As everyone was oohhing and ahhhing over Katie, I noticed Amy standing in the middle of all the legs, looking up at the smiling faces. She looked so small and so left out. I knelt down beside her so that we were eye to eye with Katie between us.

"Amy? Would you like to show everyone how you can hold Katie?" I asked gently. She beamed with pride as she took Katie into her arms like an old pro. Yeah, I guess Jerry was right. She'll be fine.

And indeed, the roughness and aggression became less and less frequent in the following weeks, only to be replaced by baby talk . . . baby walk . . . baby everything. It wasn't enough to have the doll that drank a bottle, wet, and said "ma-ma." Oh, no; *she* wanted to do all those things herself! It all started with that darn baby swing. She'd clamber in it and call, "Ma-ma! Ma-ma!" in a nasal-like version of her doll. Then she'd gesture wildly at the crank and stammer, "Swing, swing," which actually sounded more like, "Fwing, fwing." I'd bite my tongue, put on a false smile, and say, "Oh, look! Baby wants to swing! Here we go, baby. Here we go up in the swing." And I'd crank the thing up, give it a shove, and leave the room muttering, "I can't believe she is doing this. It's so revolting!" And it was. I'm sorry to say, but I was disgusted with her moronic stagger, her absurd baby talk, and her constant need to include me in her baby play.

"Let's say I cry and you give me a rattle," she'd say. Or "Let's say I fuss and you have to rub my back." So she did and I would, but I didn't enjoy it. And understanding why she was doing it didn't really make it any easier to live with. It should have, but it didn't. Obviously she wanted the same attention Katie was getting and therefore figured she was better off as a baby than as a big sister. I could relate to that, but it still irritated the pants off me. My only retaliation was to put certain limitations on her "baby time."

"You can be a baby until we go to the store," I'd say. Or "Well, if you're going to be a baby now, you have to be a big girl when Grandma comes."

What she really wanted to do was drink from a baby bottle, but I just couldn't bring myself to allow it. As a compromise she used the plastic pink milk carton that came with her Fisher-Price shopping cart. It was square with a kind of spout at the top that she could chew on. While it was the least offensive thing I could think of at the time, it still made my stomach lurch whenever I saw her crawling across the floor with her "bottle" clenched between her teeth.

Then one night when Jerry was bathing Amy, she slipped into her baby routine. Wallowing around on her back, she flailed her arms aimlessly and made a series of monosyllabic sounds.

"What's happening?" Jerry asked her.

"Me baby," she drooled.

"Oh, I see. Kind of a big baby, aren't you?" Overhearing this conversation, I called to the two of them. "No baby in the bath! You were baby at dinner!"

"Mom says 'no baby,' kiddo," Jerry explained to Amy.

She started to cry, "But I didn't get to be a baby in the *bath!*"

I came into the bathroom to clarify things. "You used up your baby time at dinner. You know the rules." I mean, I spoon-fed the kid her entire meal, for crying out loud! How many other parents would do that? Enough was enough, right? She continued to cry.

"It's okay, Julie. I'll play baby with her if she wants to so badly," Jerry gave in. "What do I do?"

"That's not the point. I hate this baby thing, so I worked out a system that just might save my sanity. Otherwise she'd be baby all day long!"

"I see. Well, she hasn't done baby with me today, so we'll say that she can have five minutes of baby with me every day."

"Fine. Why not make it ten?" I smiled a kind of sick smile. What was happening to me?

"Okay, ten."

"You'll be sorry," I said and closed the bathroom door so as not to hear the *goos* and *gaas* of the game.

Baby (the *real* one) Katie was just beginning to fidget as I came back into the kitchen. I placed her infant seat on the counter so we could "talk" while I did the dishes. She was such a good baby. I leaned over and planted a squeaky kiss on her soft cheek. "Who are you anyway?" I asked out loud. She was six weeks old. By the time Amy was that age we had already probed deep into her personality. But this time I couldn't get away from my concern over Amy's bruised ego long enough to fully focus in on Katie. I reached down and pulled her out of her seat. She started involuntarily and then relaxed in my arms. Her small but solid shape felt good against my chest, and I leaned my cheek against the top of her head. "Hang in there, kid," I said to her. "We'll talk soon." I laid her back down, pulling a Winnie-the-Pooh blanket snugly around her. The same blanket, in fact, that I had tucked around Amy when she was a baby. And the realization that it really wasn't that long ago loosened the knot in my stomach and saw me through the evening.

Amy wet her bed that night. And every night after that for a week. Having been a bed-wetter myself, and at a much older age than hers, I was not one to accuse or scold, but by the end of the week it was getting pretty old. So we talked; we eliminated liquids after six-thirty and I even carried her to the bathroom before going to bed myself after Katie's ten-o'clock feeding. One night Katie woke up around two-thirty and I fed her, changed her and rocked her back to sleep, getting back into bed about three-fifteen. I had just crawled under the covers of my own bed and begun to drift back to sleep when I heard Amy's whimpers. I lay in the dark, staring at the ceiling, unable to tear myself away from the warmth and comfort of my bed. Jerry, of course, slept soundlessly on.

"Damn!" I muttered, just loud enough to wake him, and threw back the covers to ensure that he knew I was getting up, *again*.

"What's the matter?" he asked sleepily.

"Oh, it's Amy. She's probably wet her bed again."

"Do you want me to go?" It was a pathetically weak offer. He only asked so that I couldn't grumble later that he didn't help in the night. "I tried," he would say, "but you wouldn't let me." Which would be true; irritating, but true.

So I groped my way up the stairs and followed the glow of the nightlight into Amy's room. In the dim light I could see her sitting up in bed. I walked over to her and slipped my hand under the covers. Sheets, pads, blankets—the works were soaked through.

"I wet my bed," she said simply. It was what she always said.

"Amy," I said wearily, "what are we going to do about this?"

"I don't know," came her reply.

I stripped the bed and rummaged around in the dark for new covers.

"I know you're not doing this on purpose, Amy, but it has to stop!" And then, because I was tired, tired and disappointed, I said sarcastically, "Maybe you should wear diapers to bed again." It was a mean thing to say but, then, at three-thirty in the morning I felt like being mean. But it was also stupid.

"Okay," she answered.

Oh, wonderful, I thought. I really set myself up for that one. She'd love nothing more than to wear diapers to bed—the ultimate in playing baby!

"Well, guess again!" I snapped while frantically thinking of a way around my unfortunate remark. "Diapers are for babies, Amy. And as much as you may hate to admit it, *you* are not a baby. You are almost three years old, and you need to accept that and be proud of what a big girl you've become."

"But can I still play baby sometimes?" Oh, that was *so* Amy. She never let anything go by; she always had a last word.

"I suppose." I sighed. I slipped a clean nightgown over her head, and she climbed back into bed, her knees making deep creases in the fresh sheets. "Good night," I said, kissing her lightly on the forehead.

"Good night, Mommy."

Back in bed, Jerry asked, "Did she wet her bed again?"

"Of course. And when I said she ought to wear diapers at night she actually liked the idea. How sick."

"Well, considering her recent behavior, it was probably a pretty dumb thing to suggest."

"Oh, I fully agree, but I was upset and, hey, I didn't see you up there changing sheets. . . ."

"I—"

"I know, I know, you offered to go." See? Works every time. "It's just that this isn't how I imagined it would be. I mean, I expected to be tired and I was prepared for jealousy, but I never thought Amy'd be such a basket case. It's a terrible disappointment, really. That sounds selfish, doesn't it?"

"No, it sounds natural. Look, if you're that bothered by all this baby stuff, why don't you talk to someone about it?"

"I suppose I could ask Maggie. She's been through this with Amanda. I'll see how tomorrow goes."

By ten the next day I had, indeed, decided to seek outside help. While I was able to postpone her "baby play" for several hours, by the time *Sesame Street* was over she was chomping at the bit.

"*Now* can we play baby?" she pleaded.

"Okay," I said, "you can be baby for a little while." At first she was content to crawl around the living room, pulling herself up on things and groping her way along tables. Then we played with Katie's baby toys and rocked in the rocking chair. When I told her it was time for her to get dressed for our walk before lunch, she begged me to dress her like she was a baby. Still feeling guilty over last night's scene, I went along with the idea. As I struggled to clothe her wiggling body, tugging this way and that at her pants, I decided to seek some second opinions.

What the Books Said

I thumbed through Dr. Spock and found a section entitled "Managing Young Children." Right below this it read,
"Jealousy and Rivalry." I flipped to page 340. Aha! Listen
to this: "A great majority of young children react to a baby's
arrival by yearning to be a baby again, at least part of the
time, and this is quite normal. They want a bottle occasionally. They may wet their bed and pants, and they may soil
themselves. They may relapse into baby talk and act helpless about doing things for themselves." Dr. Spock went on
to say, "I think a parent is wise to humor the craving to be a
baby *at those moments* when it is very strong. They can
even good-naturedly carry a child up to his room and
undress him, as a friendly game." While on the one hand I
felt good that I had been doing what he suggested, I was
also a touch disappointed. I think I had secretly hoped that
he would condemn the regression back to baby. He did go
on to say, though, that "parents can help the child more by
appealing, most of the time, to the side of him that wants to
grow up [and] remind him of how big, strong, smart or
skillful he is." Well, it made sense and sounded simple
enough, but then Dr. Spock wasn't the one who'd been
changing the bedsheets every night. I felt better, though,
knowing that her babyish behavior was normal. Dr. Spock
even said to let the older child drink from a bottle, that "he'll
only want it occasionally and give it up soon as long as you
help him with his jealous feelings." I felt a stab of guilt as I
pictured Amy chewing on the pink plastic milk carton
because I couldn't handle her drinking from a real bottle. So
what's the bottom line, then? Be patient, it'll pass?

I decided to check out *The Mother's Almanac*. And while
there was no mention of an older child's urge to be a baby
again, Ms. Kelly and Ms. Parsons did write, "When you

have a new baby, you may be ashamed of your love—not the rather prosaic love you feel for your newborn—but the overwhelming love you feel for your first child. . . . It will take months for your newborn to find his niche, and until he does, he won't know what he's missing." That made me feel better. I thought they might have something further to say about regression, but the index went from Records to Renovation. So I gave up and took a shot at Joan Beck's *Effective Parenting*.

Here again was the idea that even though a firstborn may "fuss for a bottle or wet his pants," it was "more than likely that, with encouragement, the first born will enjoy noting his superiority and try to act even more grown up."

Throughout all these books, and others, was the advice to spend as much time alone with the older child as possible, as well as to encourage him to help you with the baby. Actually none of this was news to me. But it was reassuring to know that bedwetting, baby talk, and bottle sucking were all natural ways children had of handling this situation. Knowing this, I softened toward Amy and even gave her some extra "baby time," although I never could bring myself to "cheerfully" fix her a bottle as Dr. Spock had suggested.

What Maggie Said

I called Maggie later that day because, even though I was feeling better, I was still interested in what the voice of experience had to say.

"Julie," Maggie began after hearing my sad story, "you really can't go by me. Amanda was only eighteen months old when Megan was born. She really *was* still in diapers and drinking a bottle!"

"True," I answered. "But in some ways maybe that would be easier. At least you expected to be dealing with two babies at a time. I never thought Amy would regress so."

"Oh, but they all go through that. My sister-in-law went though the exact same thing. Let me tell you what she did. It might help. She had all these little gifts wrapped up, you know, in case someone came by with a gift for the baby but nothing for her three-year-old."

"Yeah, yeah." I sighed. "I did that, too. But how did that help? I mean, other than in the obvious way of avoiding hurt feelings?"

"It was the gifts themselves that made the difference. She bought him things that would make him feel really grown up. She wrapped up one of those notebooks, you know, the kind with a clipboard and compartments in it. An inexpensive portable radio was another gift. It was a big hit. He could take it outside, fiddle with the dials, and turn the music up as loud as he liked. And she'd say, 'We bought you this because you're such a big boy!' "

"That's a good idea."

"Yeah, and it would even be easier with a girl because you could get her fingernail polish, perfumed lotion, lipstick, all that stuff you love so." Maggie laughed.

"Yuck," I answered. Maggie knew how much I abhorred all that goop. But it would be worth sacrificing my principles to pull Amy out of her baby slump.

"Oh, and another neat thing she did was to get him some dress-up outfits. There was a cowboy hat and holster, a fireman's hat , and even a little army helmet."

"Sounds a little sexist to me," I commented. "Did he really regress that much?"

"Oh, yeah, he'd crawl around, and she'd even let him have a bottle and wear diapers."

I let out a groan.

"Yeah, I know," continued Maggie, "but after a while he preferred his dress-up stuff and new toys to playing baby."

"Your sister-in-law sounds like some kind of supermom. I think I hate her."

"Well, you ought to see her. She weighs close to a hundred and seventy-five pounds and has a mustache."

"This isn't the same sister-in-law who dropped out of law school, is it?" I asked.

"Oh, no. *That's* John's sister, Kathy. Did I tell you what happened to her?"

"No," I answered and settled back into my chair while Maggie filled me in on the latest developments of her extended family. It felt good to hear her prattle on cheerfully, and really, they were a fascinating bunch. After all, I had gotten what I had called for—advice. When Maggie finally wound down, I thanked her for her help and promised to let her know how it all worked out.

What My Mother Said

I had no sooner hung up the phone than it rang again.

"Hi, honey!" It was my mother.

"Oh, hi, Mom."

"Who were you talking to? Your line was busy forever."

"Oh, that was Maggie. We were talking about all this baby play-acting that Amy's doing. It's driving me nuts!"

"I know. It *is* gross! And you're always so sweet to her. No one would ever guess it bothered you. Really, Julie, you're so patient with Amy."

I was grateful for the compliment about being patient. Whether or not I deserved it, it made me feel good to know she had that confidence in me. But her remark about Amy's "gross" behavior stung a little.

"Well, I'm really not all that patient with her, and anyway, I didn't know Amy's baby play bugged you," I answered defensively. "You play it with her all the time." I tried not to sound too accusing, but meant it that way just the same.

"Oh, well, poor kid. It's what she wants to do, and it won't last forever. It's nothing to *me* if she wants to be baby all day, but I know how discouraged you must be. That's all, honey. I'm just sympathizing with you, not criticizing by any means."

My irritation vanished and I asked, "So you think she'll pull out of it soon?"

"Oh, I don't know about 'soon,' but it can't last too much longer. What did Maggie say?"

I told my mother about our conversation, and she thought the sister-in-law's ideas were very sensible.

"I've got a bunch of old hats and jewelry of your grandmother's. Let me bring them over this afternoon," she offered.

"Okay."

"And then we ought to take her some place special for lunch this weekend. Just the three of us. Jerry can stay with Katie, and we'll treat Amy to a 'girls' day out'! How does that sound?"

"It sounds fun. She'd like that, I'm sure. We'll have her so grown up she'll be asking to use the car if we're not careful!" I laughed.

"That'll be the day. But don't push her, Julie," my mother warned. "Let her have her baby time, too. I mean that."

"I know, I know. . . ."

"Hang in there and I'll be by later."

"'Bye, Mom."

Amy was just waking from her nap when I got off the phone. As soon as I entered her room, she rolled over on her back and cried, *"Wa, wa, wa,"* pounding the bed with her fists and feet.

"Baby hungry," she informed me.

I ignored this remark and said, "Would you like to put on your fancy shoes and I'll push you in the swing?"

"Okay!" she answered cheerfully. "We'll pretend I'm a baby swinging."

Any old time, Mom, I thought to myself.

What My Husband Said

Later that evening Jerry's mother called and when he finally hung up the phone I asked, "So what did your mom have to say?"

"Oh, I was just filling her in on Amy's passion for playing baby. She thinks it's quite clever of her."

"Clever?" I said sharply. "Clever? Clever is hiding in the clothes hamper during a game of hide-and-go-seek, clever is decorating orange slices with raisin eyes. Cats that can open doors with their little paws are clever, but, trust me, three-years-olds who crawl around saying *'goo goo'* are *not* clever!"

"No, I don't suppose they are," Jerry answered calmly. "But regardless of how irritating Amy is or how disappointing her behavior may be, you've got to keep in mind that you're the adult and she's the child."

"You always say things like that. Well, I don't want to be the adult. I'm tired of doing what's best, being patient, and thinking of myself last. What I'd really like to do is have a tantrum!" I snapped. Being irrational was my best defense against his cool, logical answers. It made us even. And once he made his precise points and I my illogical accusations, we could move ahead and discuss things in a more civilized manner.

"I thought you were going to talk to Maggie about this baby stuff," he said. His voice had lost its articulate edge and he was looking at me closely. I knew he was thinking that I was overtired; Katie was still waking in the night, but he was afraid to say anything that might sound condescending for fear I would become even more riled up. I decided to let the poor guy off the hook. He worked hard, too.

"Yes, I did, and she had some interesting suggestions." And then I added, "I didn't mean to snap at you; it's just that I'm tired. . . ."

"Oh, darn," he interrupted with a smile. "Does this mean you're not going to have your tantrum? I was looking forward to seeing that. Do you lie on the floor and kick, or are you a door-slammer?" We were both laughing now. "I'll tell you what, why don't you see if your mother can come over tomorrow night and watch the kids so we can go out to dinner. It's been a long time since we've been out, just the two of us. And as far as Amy goes, follow up on Maggie's ideas, but, as much as I hate to say this, I think my mother was right—Amy *is* clever; we just have to be cleverer!"

I had the feeling that this was going to be the story of our lives.

What I Did

Amy was in heaven with Grandma's old hats and necklaces, and there were even some bracelets and purses that added an elegant touch. For several days there was no sign of "baby Amy" at all, but as the newness of the costumes wore off, playing baby crept back into her regular routine.

So when I took my film in to be developed at the drugstore, I picked up a few trinkets made especially for "growing little girls" (ugh). There were nail polishes ranging in color from shocking pink to golden glitter, bubble bath, powder puffs, and perfumed lotion. I chose a modest pink polish (the closest thing to clear I could find), some bubble bath, lotion, and a gloved powder mitt that seemed harmless enough. I couldn't bring myself to buy lipstick, but I found a strawberry Chapstick that would serve the same purpose.

Amy was thrilled with her beauty aids. She lavishly applied the lotion to her bony legs and delicately stroked the pink polish onto finger and toe nails. The house reeked of imitation lilac, and there was even some talk of hair curlers. At this point I wasn't sure which was more revolting, the overgrown baby or this walking glamour gal. I had created a monster!

And when we occasionally took Amy out to lunch or to a show, she was obviously proud and pleased to be the big sister. But it was the passage of time that really got us through. The diversions helped; they helped show Amy it was fun to be a big girl, too. And they gave that compulsive side of me some action to take while time ticked away. Shopping for toiletries and playing tea party made me feel that I was doing my best to help Amy.

3

The Trial
of a Tadpole

There's a growing phenomenon out here in California called the swimming lesson. It may even be sweeping the nation like soccer or Strawberry Shortcake, for all I know. But I *do* know that each year in May, when the various recreation departments distribute their summer program schedules, mothers begin marking the appropriate box for the date, day, and session of their choice. You see, there is something for everyone in swimming. First of all, you've got your "Mommy and Me" classes. These are for the littlest of little ones, anywhere from three months to three years old. "Tadpoles" (not an altogether flattering term, but philosophically sound) are a step up from "Mommy and Me" and are composed of preschool children. And then the more traditional levels of "Beginner," "Intermediate," and so forth take over.

Now, "Mommy and Me" is harmless enough. I mean, you get in the water, make bubbles, bob around, blow on the baby's face, and do a quick dunk or two. Most babies

46

like it fine. Mom holds them nice and close, the water rushes through their toes, and, hey, any occasion that calls for diaperlessness is a welcome one! Oh, there are always a few criers, just as there are overachievers who leap fearlessly from the side, but everyone is understanding, and an acceptable option is always to sit on the steps and let your baby acquaint herself with the water's texture, or pull, or push, or some such thing. Even when she climbs out of the pool and runs away, you can say you're helping her explore the surrounding sights and sounds so she'll feel more comfortable in her environment. Yes, they let you get away with a lot in "Mommy and Me." It's nice.

But this story is about a Tadpole, and when you're a Tadpole life gets a little tougher. The experts say that three is supposed to be an easy age, a period of equilibrium, if you will, but for us, three was a difficult neither-here-nor-there stage. I mean, we had lived through the terrible twos, which really began around fifteen months, and looming in the distance was the outrageously foolish behavior of the four-year-old who has discovered the impact of bathroom words, so this was our big chance for some normalcy, right? And, no longer in diaper, stroller, crib, or highchair, Amy seemed so grown-up, so ready to forge ahead into the brave new world. And goodness knows there's everything from tap dancing and tumbling to roller-skating and ballet available to a three-year-old. So the spring before Amy's third birthday I headed up to the high school pool along with all the other mothers, to register Amy as a Tadpole. It never occurred to me that my expectation of being "home free" for a while might be setting me up for a fall.

The first day Amy was fine. Glenn, a young, blond instructor, let the parents sit down by the pool because it was the first day.

"But," he forewarned us, "after today you'll have to say goodbye to your child at the gate. You can go around and watch from the bleachers if you want, but sit up at the top and please don't interrupt the class." He said this with the assurance of someone who knew what he was talking about. Hey, fine with me. I looked forward to sitting back and enjoying the show. So on that first day we sat by the pool while Glenn lifted the children into the water, telling them to blow bubbles, kick their legs, or reach for rings. Out of the six in the class only two became quite unstrung as they were lowered into the pool. The little girl's mother explained to the rest of us that her daughter, Tiffany, had had an ear infection and was overtired. I was embarrassed for her. Somehow it was no longer acceptable to make those excuses the way we all did in "Mommy and Me." All that nonsense about texture and environment, no one really believed it, but we all went along with it because there was still plenty of time to grow up. I guess time starts to run out around three, though, because that's when we expect our kids to get their acts together. At least I did. But while I knew that Tiffany's mother was covering up for her, I didn't know how ashamed she was that she felt the need to do it. The other crier was Greg, a small, fair-haired boy in over-sized red trunks. His mother said nothing at all. I wouldn't be feeling superior to these women for long.

Jerry took Amy to her next lesson. I quizzed him later in my usual fashion, and he responded in his usual noncommittal way.

"So how did she do?"

"Fine. They didn't do too much. It's only a half an hour."

"Well, did she put her face in the water?"

"Yeah, I guess so."

"What do you mean, you guess so? Weren't you watching?"

"Well, I was way up on those bleachers, and then I ran into Dan Pratt. You remember, he taught biology when we were at the high school."

"Oh, yeah. He's still there?"

"Uh-huh, only he's a counselor now. He was filling me in on everyone from the old days."

"Well, anyway, did that little Tiffany cry? She's got that long ponytail and wears a blue suit."

"I don't know, maybe. Someone was crying down there. But Mr. Pratt told me that his son was teaching out by us and—"

"It wasn't Amy, was it?"

"What do you mean?"

"Crying. Did Amy cry?"

"Oh, no, she was fine. Do you want to hear about Dan Pratt or not?"

Hopeless. How could a person go to watch his child, on her own for the first time, and not pay attention? I wanted to ask him if she had followed instructions, talked to the teacher or other kids at all, jumped from the side. Hopeless. Well, he would be at work tomorrow and I could take her.

I should have sensed trouble when Amy awoke at six the next morning and came in to ask if today was Swimming.

"Yes! Right after *Sesame Street*. Okay?" No answer. I didn't like the feel of it. Uncomfortable thoughts started to push their way into my mind. I decided to change the subject.

"Is your sister up yet, or is she a sleepyhead this morning?" I asked.

"Oh, she's up. I heard her goo-gooing in there." Big smile. We were going to be okay.

A little before ten o'clock Amy's grandma arrived. She'd volunteered to stay with Kate while Amy had her lesson. Amy put on her suit and we set off for the high school. As we neared the pool Amy said, "You stay and watch."

"Oh, I will. But I have to go up on those bleachers, like Daddy did."

"I want you to stay down by me."

"Well, I can't, honey. Glenn said it's a rule. Moms watch from up above." We approached the gate. "Here, give me a quick kiss and off you go!" As Amy reached her arms up to give me a hug, I knew I had made a major mistake. I could almost hear her fingers locking into an ironclad grip behind my neck.

Using a phony everything-is-fine voice, I said, "Okay, honey. Enough hugs. Let's go now. There's Glenn!" Her grip loosened as she turned to see if Glenn was indeed coming, and I took advantage of this momentary distraction. Slipping out of her grip, I made a fast retreat to the bleachers.

Tiffany and the boy, Greg, started crying right away. When Amy started into her heart-wrenching "I want my mommy!" I heard myself saying, "I think they get each other all hyped up. She was fine yesterday. Well, she's been up since six o'clock. Probably ready for a nap." First I felt the embarrassment and knew they all felt it too; then I felt the shame. I wanted to look at Tiffany's mom, I wanted to say something to her about how it feels and how senseless it was for us to pretend with each other. I wanted to ask her what she was going to do. But I couldn't bring myself to make eye contact. I mean, we've trained ourselves to avoid the stares of those crabby old ladies in markets and irritable sales clerks in Bullock's that cluck their tongues at naughty children or even loud children or just children in general. Old habits die hard.

Meanwhile Amy's cries continued, with momentary inter-ruptions only when it was her turn to swim. It was one of the longest half-hours of my life, comparable only to the last half-hour of a ten-hour car trip with the kids or the half-hour you spend with a two-year-old in the doctor's office trying not to scrunch up the paper on the little bed.

When Jerry came home from work that afternoon, Amy was playing with her eighteen-inch baby doll, Vicki.

"C'mon, Vicki, do your big arms. I'm right here. Don't be scared." Then there was a horrible sobbing as Amy pulled poor Vicki across the living room flapping her arms up and down.

"Wa, wa, wa!" cried Amy for Vicki.

"Shhh, you're okay," answered Amy, now the teacher.

"What's all that about?" asked Jerry, indicating the scene in the living room.

"I don't want to talk about it. I am so depressed." Pause. "She cried all through her lesson today. Sobbed, 'I want my mommy,' while I sat up on those stupid bleachers and pretended not to hear. It was a nightmare. Now look at her. She's been dragging Vicki across the carpeting, making her do her "big arms" for the last half-hour. Wait until you see Amy make her jump off the coffee table. It's pathetic."

"I thought you didn't want to talk about it."

"Oh, sure, go ahead and act smug, just because she didn't cry when you took her."

"I'm not acting smug, and she'll probably be fine tomor-row."

"I doubt it. She'll probably start crying before we even get there, and then I'll have to drag her to the pool kicking and screaming. God, I'm depressed."

"So don't go."

"You see! That's what I hate about telling you this stuff. You just say, 'So don't go,' like it's all that simple."

"Well, it *is*."

"No, it's not! She was fine the first two days, you saw that. Now she pulls this freak-out stuff, just to drive me nuts, I swear. If she quits now she'll have gotten her way. She'll think that any time she puts up a fuss we'll let her off the hook. She'll be a quitter all her life. Is that what you want? *Plus* she'll feel she's failed, and it could weaken her self-esteem!"

"Seems to me you've already worked this whole thing out. Then make her go."

"Easy for you to say."

"Julie, what do you want me to say? I only—"

"Oh, God, there she goes. Watch."

Vicki stood on the coffee table facing Amy, who held her around the waist. "C'mon, Vicki. Jump to me! You can do it."

"No! I want my mommy! I want my mommy!" Amy responded for Vicki. One eye drooped half shut on the doll, and there was a smudge of dirt on her cheek that only made the scene that much more pitiful. Suddenly Amy flung Vicki face down on the carpeting and pulled her across the floor by her arms.

"Good girl! Now it's Tiffany's turn."

Jerry and I had watched the scenario in silence.

"Don't you think that's weird?" I asked.

"Well, I don't know. Maybe it helps her to work out her feelings. You notice she *does* make Vicki jump in. That must mean something. Anyway, you get too worked up over these things. What's for dinner?"

I asked my mother to take Amy to her Thursday lesson. She knew all about Amy's problem and agreed that things might go more smoothly without me. I had high hopes for this plan of action and awaited their return anxiously.

Amy came through the door first, looking a little shaken. She didn't answer when I asked how her lesson went. My heart sank.

"Oh! Julie! How did you stand it?" My mother rushed into the house.

"What?" As if I didn't know.

"The sobs and calls for help. It was heartbreaking."

"Oh, no . . . she did it *again?* With you?"

"I would have pulled her out of that pool like a shot, but I was afraid you'd be mad at me. I went and sat in the car, with the windows rolled up."

"Oh, Mom, I'm sorry. I thought she'd be better with you. Did she cry the whole time?"

"Started at the gate. I couldn't get her to let go of my leg."

"Don't tell me any more." Such a wave of disappointment and despondency had washed over me that I felt drained.

"Look, honey, I have to go or I'll be late for my hair appointment. Are you going to be all right?"

"Yeah, go ahead, and thanks for taking her. Now at least I know it isn't just me."

"It isn't that big a deal, Julie. She'll live. Why don't you go read her a book or play something quiet before Kate wakes up? Don't bug her about the lessons, though. Hang in there!" She closed the door quietly behind her as she left the room.

I walked down the hall to Amy's room. She was sitting on the floor with her back to me. I had countless photographs of that small back, strong and straight. She was lining up people from her Fisher-Price playhouse.

"Can I play?" I asked.

"Sure, you be the farm."

I began to set up my fences and barnyard animals. "So how was swimming?" Damn! I wasn't going to do that!

"I cried."

"Why?"

"I wanted Grandma to come down there."

"Did she?"

"No."

"So there's no point in crying, is there?"

Amy just shrugged her shoulders. I didn't feel any better having discussed it, but I just couldn't stop myself. "Well, it's not fair to do that to Grandma. She wanted to see you swim." That's right, add guilt to all the poor kid's problems. I must be really sick. Feeling thoroughly disgusted with myself, I loaded up my wagon with animals and headed over to Amy's "house" for a visit.

And that afternoon she played "swimming lessons" again, dragging Vicki's stuffed body across the carpet time after time.

Day five. Six o'clock A.M. "Is today Swimming?"

There was that ghostly figure at my bedside again. She stood with her hair all askew and looked at me with eyes still soft from sleep. God, they can break your heart, can't they?

"Climb in here, sweetheart, and cuddle with me."

She did. Her soft, warm body nestled next to mine. "You know I love you, Amy." And I did. It was so overwhelming when it caught me off guard like that. It just filled me up until I thought I'd either explode or cry. And I stroked her small head, feeling guilty that I didn't love her like this all the time. But kids are easier to love in the morning before they've done anything to irritate you. And just then I wasn't irritated—if anything, I felt sorry for her. She was so small, trying to cope with feelings so powerful. I held her close to me, wrapping my protective arms around her. If only it were this simple, I thought. I could handle those more primitive needs of food, shelter, warmth, and protection. I would be good at that. It's all this decision making that makes things tough. I should've been an animal. I'd make a great she-bear.

Amy broke my thoughts. "Is there Swimming today?"

"Yes."

"I don't want to go."

"Why?"

After a brief pause she answered, "I don't want you to sit so far away."

"Well, I have to, honey."

"I don't want you to."

"Well, that's where I sit, and you're going to be fine today. No tears. So let's just forget about crying and have a good time. Okay? Good. You think you could help me make some cookies this morning?"

"Yes, but I don't want to go to swimming."

I was irritated. Six-ten in the morning and already I was irritated. If only I could save a few good thoughts to tap into later on today. I would try. Really try.

The chanting started just after we got in the car.

"I don't want to go. I don't want to go."

I tried to take a firm-but-understanding position and answered, "I hear what you're saying and I understand that you're upset. But today is Swimming and you will be fine." I think if anyone were to say that to me in a smug tone of voice, I'd scream!

When we got there, Tiffany's mother was talking to Glenn, ". . . we may try again later on in the summer, but I just don't think she's ready."

"Are you sure?" Glenn asked.

"Yes, I appreciate your help but she gets so upset and it's hard for you to help the others."

"Well, listen, I look forward to seeing her later on, then. 'Bye!"

I was impressed. She did that with such ease and confidence. I wondered if it were really that easy for her. I mean, did *she* worry that Tiffany had "gotten her way"? I would like to have talked to her, but I had problems of my own just then.

I had nudged Amy toward Glenn and the pool, but she wailed, "I didn't get a *kiss!*" at the last minute.

Wearing a cheerful smile I didn't feel, I said, "Oh! Forgot the kiss! Well, come here." But this time I was prepared and caught her hands in mine before she could trap me. Our eyes met. We exchanged I-know-that-you-know-that-I-know looks. And I thought to myself, "I'm never going to get away with this."

"Just swim, Amy." I hissed at her. "Quit all these stupid hysterics and get in the pool and *swim!*"

I stomped out of the pool area. As I turned to close the gate, I saw Amy square her shoulders, lift her chin, and walk stoically to the pool's edge. There was that back again, strong and straight. Feeling like a real heel, I climbed to the top of the bleachers.

"Oh, dear, here we go again," was my offhand remark to Greg's mother as I sat down beside her.

"Oh, they always cry the first week. My older boy did the same thing," she answered coolly. Greg was already sobbing as he clung to the edge of the pool.

"Really?" I couldn't think of anything else to say. Tiffany's mother knew enough to quit, and Greg's mother knew enough to stay. I didn't even know enough to keep my mouth shut.

Amy was quiet for about the first ten minutes, just long

enough for me to be lulled into a false sense of security. Then she called, "Mommy! My nose is running!" I rummaged around in my purse looking for a tissue. All I could find was one of Kate's baby socks. Oh, well, it would do. I sidestepped my way down the bleachers and circled around to the gate. When I got to the edge of the pool, I leaned down to wipe Amy's nose with the sock.

"Stay down here, Mommy," she pleaded.

"I only came down to wipe your nose." As I turned to leave, Amy began to cry harder than ever.

"Mommy, don't leave! Mommy, don't leave!"

I couldn't face climbing back up those bleachers to sit with the other mothers chatting about vacation plans and children's shoes, so I stood to the side of the bleachers.

"Mommy, where are you?" was Amy's next desperate wail. Apparently she knew right where I had been sitting.

"Right over here." I called.

"Come here. Please! I need you!"

I thought about going to the car.

"I have to go to the bathroom!" she screamed. It was a stroke of genius. Who could deny a child a trip to the bathroom even when we all knew it was just a trick? And believe me, there was no doubt in anyone's mind that this was a trick. Reeling under the emotional blows she was dealing me, I staggered back around to the pool. I pulled her silently from the water. Her small, firm body shivered in the cool morning air.

"Get your towel," I said coldly. Once inside the restroom I yanked down her suit and plunked her on a toilet seat.

"So go," I said.

"I don't have to," she answered.

I kneeled down on the cold cement slab in front of her. Her bathing suit dangled from her ankles and she whimpered, "Please don't make be go back." I hated her and I loved her. I wanted to slap her and to hold her. And taking the whole thing personally, I said all the wrong things.

"Why are you doing this to me? Why can't you swim like everyone else? What's wrong with you?"

By the time we pulled ourselves together, class was just ending.

"Okay, kids, everybody out for today. See you all Monday!" Glenn called.

We had some serious thinking to do before Monday.

What the Books Said

I learned more than I ever wanted to know about egg-shaped bubbles versus inflatable arm bands in the great life-preserver controversy before I finally found something of interest in *The Mother's Almanac*. The swimming entry in the index referred me to "Coordination, skills of," and from there I ended up on page 65. Here the authors recommended that "the sooner you give your child the chance to swim, the quicker he'll take to the water." But there was no mention of what to do if he doesn't want to "take to the water." They did say, however, that even at four a child is afraid to go underwater, and not to really expect them to swim until around six.

I thought *Understanding Your Child from Birth to Three* might be of some help since it details those early years, but the index hopped from "Sucking, need of" to "Symbolic realism" (I hope I never have *that* problem, whatever it is!), so I went on to *Kids: Day In and Day Out*. I was pleasantly surprised to find a section entitled "Teaching Kids to Swim: Conflicting Theories." First was a short article by John Holt (author of *How Children Learn*) describing his own personal experience in teaching his daughter, who was quite fearful, to swim. His comment was, "If we continually try to force a child to do what he is afraid to do, he will become more timid and will use his brains and energy not to explore the unknown but to find ways to avoid the pressures we put on him. If, however, we are careful not to push a child beyond the limits of his courage, he is almost sure to get braver." That sounded pretty good to me.

The next article was by Alan Saperstein, who told the story of *his* six-year-old's first swimming lesson. In this story the hysterical son was dunked repeatedly by the instructor. Mr. Saperstein tells how he left the scene feeling upset and guilty, but upon his return his son was proudly kicking across the pool on a Styrofoam board. Interesting, but keep in mind that the boy was *six,* and he settled down after the first day.

From all this I got the idea that while there were definitely two schools of thought on the subject, there was also an assumption that you didn't try to teach real swimming until after four years old. But even if my daughter was too young, I felt that my problem was probably one of separation and even manipulation as much as it was of swimming readiness. Then I found a comforting thought in Joan Beck's *Effective Parenting.* In her section on nursery school she says that the parent should "reserve the right to reconsider nursery school" if the child is crying, having tantrums, or claiming to be sick on school mornings. She continues, "Chances are, in another six months or a year he'll welcome the experience he's rejecting now—if you don't force it on him now, when he's not ready." There was no mention of permanent character damage or anything!

I couldn't find anything in Dr. Spock, but to be perfectly honest I got bogged down in the weaning-from-breast-to-cup section. After all, I had Kate to consider too, and I always thought that sounded like a terrific idea, eliminating the bottle and all. Anyway I had all weekend to think over what I had read.

What Maggie Said

I knew that Maggie had signed Amanda up for lessons, but I never did hear how it went. The lessons would be over, though, because I remember her saying she could only do it the last week in May. That way she'd have time to do a "Mommy and Me" session with eighteen-month-old Megan before the new baby was born in July. She was really going to have her hands full. But then, if anyone could do it, Maggie could. She's got her priorities pretty well set. The kids come first, but she's got her own self-esteem running a close second. She'll sit surrounded by rubble and read clear through the *Los Angeles Times*. She knows more about the problems in the Middle East and labor union disputes than any other friend I have. And it doesn't bother her at all that last night's dishes are still sitting in the sink. But for now, I only wanted to hear about the swimming lessons and hoped to avoid any long-winded discussion on air traffic control.

"Hi, Maggie, it's me, Julie. How're you feeling?"

"Oh, fine. I'm carrying the baby so low this time! I even had some false labor last week. The doctor said he might do a pelvic next visit. I think I must be dilated at least two centimeters." Maggie loved being pregnant and having babies. She would discuss sore nipples, hemorrhoids, and mucus plugs the way other people discuss baby names, due dates, and crib styles. Hey, it's the gift of life, right?

"Well, you're getting right down to the wire. Listen, I called to see how Amanda liked her swimming lessons. Amy's taking hers now and hates them." It's best to be right up front with your friends. It takes the pressure off them. Now Maggie could afford to be generous instead of defensive about her own swimming experience.

"Oh, well, Amanda cried. She really wasn't too thrilled with them."

"Maggie, I'm talking hysterical here, I'm talking six-o'clock-in-the-morning I-don't-want-to-go-stuff."

"Really? That surprises me. Amy always seems so much more outgoing than Amanda."

"Well, you wouldn't have recognized her today. Do you think I should make her keep going?" I came right to the point.

"Oh, I would. Look, Julie, you can't let her jerk you around like that. She's got, what, five more lessons?"

"Yeah."

"Okay, you tell her she has five more lessons before her class is over. You tell her that you and Jerry decided that she will go to those lessons. Then, don't mention it again. And that's the hard part."

"You're not kidding. *She* keeps bringing it up. You should see her role-play the whole thing with her doll."

"Just ignore it. If she asks, just repeat what I said before—you decided she will go. Julie, let her know you're in charge."

"Then you don't think they're too young for swimming lessons?" I asked, thinking about what I had read.

"No, not really. And anyway, you've already started."

"But Maggie, she calls to me during the lessons, 'I have to go to the bathroom, my nose is running'. . . ."

"Oh, dear, you are having a time of it. Sit in the car. Why torture yourself?"

"I guess you're right. It won't kill her to go five more days. It may kill *me,* but she'll survive, right?"

"Julie, listen, my advice is to put yourself in charge. She's got you on the run, and I'll bet she knows it." I thought about the scenario in the pool rest room, and about the way we exchange looks . . . yeah, you can bet she knew it. "Make a decision and stick to it," Maggie finished.

"Okay, I will. Thanks a lot."

"Listen, I've got to go. I hear Megan waking up from her nap. Hang in there and let me know how it all works out. Really, Julie, if swimming lessons turn out to be our biggest problems, we must be doing *something* right!"

We hung up and I thought about what she had said. I really did need to get back in charge of this situation. But another five days . . .

What My Mother Said

I could tell when I called that my mother had been dying to put in her two cents.

"You'd be nuts to make her go back. What's the point?"

"Well, Maggie was saying that I needed to show Amy I was 'in charge' and not to let her 'jerk me around.' "

"Oh, for heaven's sake, if anyone's being jerked around it's Amy. The poor kid's a nervous wreck!"

"Maybe she's a wreck because she feels too in control of the situation and that's what's making her nervous."

"Well, you do what you feel is best, and I don't mean to criticize, but I just think she's too little for all this stuff. She's barely three, you know, and she sees Kate and me all snuggled down at home while she's got to go off to this lesson. I don't blame her. You need to give her more time."

"Yeah, but I worry about giving in. Especially with her. You know how she is, so determined. I don't know. I'll talk to Jerry tonight."

Her voice softened, "I know you think I'm too easy on

her, but really and truly you and Jerry treat her so old sometimes. It's easier for me to see how little she is. I've seen how fast children grow up. I'd like to keep her little always."

Tears sprang to my eyes, and I had to control the shakiness in my voice. "Now I feel so mean." The thought slipped out.

"Oh, honey, don't. You're a good mother. A much better mother than *I* ever was, I can tell you that!"

"Oh, sure!" I felt better, though.

"No, really, I didn't do half for you kids what you do for those two darling girls. Listen, here's my advice to you. Just drop the whole thing. Tell her the lessons are over and don't harp on it. Don't let Jerry 'discuss' it with her either. You guys talk to her too much. Now, put it out of your head. Why don't you plan to have dinner here Sunday? We'll barbecue. Jerry likes that."

"Sure. Okay, Mom. And thanks."

What My Husband Said

When confronted with "You have to help me with this, I don't know what to do," Jerry, as usual, rose to the occasion.

"First of all, you have to decide how important this swimming is to you," he began in a matter-of-fact voice.

"I do?"

"Of course. Julie, you need to pick your issues carefully. Don't put yourself through agony over something you don't even think is all that important. Save your strength for something bigger."

"But I've already picked my issue, whether I want it or

not. I mean, she's already started these stupid lessons, and I've already made a big stink about how she has to go."

"And she *did* go. And now you need to decide if learning to swim this summer is a big enough priority to make her go another five days."

"Why do *I* have to decide? Why is it always *my* problem? Why can't you just tell me what to do?" He could be so maddening.

"Because I'm not going to be the one taking her to the class. I'm not the one who signed her up in the first place."

"What is *that* supposed to mean?"

"It means I think she's too young."

"Why didn't you say so in the first place?"

"You never asked me. But that's okay. I figured you knew what you were doing, that she'd probably love it."

"Big mistake. Never assume I know what I'm doing. Any time you feel you can do things better around here, feel free to jump on in."

"That's not what I mean and you know it. I *trust* you. I trust your good judgment to know what's best for our kids. So you made a mistake. It's not the end of the world. I'm just trying to help you put things into perspective. If it were me I wouldn't do it. I wouldn't put myself through all this for swimming. She's going to learn to swim in her lifetime, we know that. If not this summer, next summer; if not that summer, then the next."

I felt a little better. That part about trust, it was nice. And he did have a way with perspective.

"But if we drop the lessons, then the next time something like this comes up she'll think she can cry her way out of it again."

"Not necessarily. She'll learn that when something is important enough, we *do* insist upon it. But we've also got to have enough flexibility to say, 'Oh, this didn't turn out to be such a good idea.' Okay?"

"I guess."

"Look at how well she goes to bed, picks up her toys, and stays on the sidewalk. Those were all situations worth the effort we put into them. Is swimming?"

What I Did

Amy didn't return to swimming on Monday. I decided to "reserve the right to reconsider." She wasn't ready . . . to swim or let go. And Jerry was right. This was not an issue I wanted to struggle over. I knew she'd never buy the line that the lessons were over, though. Hey, the kid is not stupid, and she heard Glenn say, "See you Monday." She'd go along with it, yes, but never believe it. So I said, "Amy, your father and I have decided that you won't be taking any more swimming lessons this summer. We think you should wait until next year, when you're bigger, to learn to swim." And I hoped that making it *our* decision, not hers, would reinforce the idea that we were in charge. Let's hope she bought *that!*

And the good news is, we'll never have to witness another one of Vicki's leaps from the coffee table or see her thrash out another lap across the living room rug.

4

The Basics
of a Birthday

Amy was going to be five on June 13. Wow, that seemed hard to believe. Her days of preschool and play groups would soon be behind her, and in the fall she'd enter kindergarten. This birthday seemed particularly important. The past two years hadn't been easy on Amy. Katie's birth, a move to a new house, and my switch from full-time work to full-time mom had taken their toll on her emotionally. But that was all behind her now, and she looked forward to this party as a kind of coming-of-age celebration. It had to be special.

The first thing to consider was where the gala event would take place. There are many party-type facilities available nowadays, not the least of which is the fast-food birthday extravaganza. This arrangement includes a meal consisting of hamburgers, fries, and a drink, plus a cake and party hats. A portion of the restaurant is sectioned off, and the birthday boy or girl can open presents while waiting to be served. You can even have the parents bring their children to the restaurant and then come back for them at a designated time. This setup definitely has its advantages, even if pink and orange isn't your favorite color combination.

But if hamburgers aren't your thing, you can go with pizza. Some places even have party rooms. What more could you ask, except perhaps for a few windows to shed some light into the gloomy atmosphere? Amy went to one pizza parlor where there were talking animals on all the walls, a roomful of video games, and a half dozen rides like you see outside of supermarkets: bucking broncos, rocking spaceships, and the like. What can I say? It's a tough act to follow. The noise level alone could never be beat.

And don't forget the ice-cream parlor party. There are a number of places that do birthday parties, some even with a make-your-own sundae policy. It's something to think about, anyway; that and the sugar high immediately following.

For those less food-oriented there's the skating party, ice or roller. Many rinks offer a short period of instruction to the party guests as well as cake and ice cream in the festive party room. But the individual needs and ages of your guests should be taken into account before scheduling this kind of event. And although miniature golf and bowling are birthday favorites, they should probably be reserved for older children.

And last but not least is the home party. Yes, trace the birthday party back to its origins and you'll discover that the birthday was first founded in the home. It's an unusual, if not frightening, prospect, I'll agree, but it has possibilities.

Not being my decision to make, I asked the birthday girl her opinion. "So what do you want to do for your birthday, kiddo?"

"I don't know. What would be fun?" A good question. Fun for whom?

"Well, there's McDonald's, Shakey's Pizza, Skateway, and places like that," I suggested with a heavy heart.

"No, I want to do it at home. Then we can decorate the house and put balloons on the gate," she replied thoughtfully. Balloons on the gate. How sweet. Kids are full of surprises, aren't they? I never would have guessed Amy would choose balloons on a gate over "Happy Birthday, Amy" sung over a loudspeaker. But I was pleased. I thought it showed good sense and a certain respect for tradition.

"Well, I think that sounds lovely," I said. "But if we have the party here, should we have a clown like that little boy from school, or a magician like Amanda did? Then there's ponies. You remember those ponies at Kelly's party—"

"Not the clown," Amy interrupted. "He wasn't that great."

"Oh?"

"Yeah, he had all this orange and purple hair, and no one really wanted to get very close to him."

I thought about how children love the big Smokey the Bear at the fire station and Woodsey the Owl who comes to the schools, but I could see Amy's point about the clown—not exactly what you would call huggable.

"I thought he did magic tricks," I said.

"Yeah, he did that one with the Ping Pong balls under the paper cups and some other stuff with a scarf, but it was kind of boring."

"Boring! Well, no one will *dare* call this party boring! The clown is O-U-T out!" I joked.

"Oh, Mom," Amy feigned embarrassment.

"Well, what about that magician? Was he fun?"

"Yeah, he was pretty good, but I kept raising my hand to be an assistant and he never called on me." I could see that this had soured the experience for her. As the act continued she had probably put more energy into her hand-raising than into enjoying the show. Well, that problem could be resolved by drawing names from a hat or something.

"We can keep it in mind, anyway. What about those ponies? Did you enjoy that?"

"That was okay, except the ponies walked so slowly. After a while it got . . ." She flashed me a laughing look and we said in unison, "Boring!" Then we cracked up. Oh, she was a cute girl! "They'd be better for Katie's next party," Amy said of the ponies when we stopped laughing.

"Well, you can only eat cake and open presents for so long. We need to plan *some* kind of activity for your guests," I said, beginning to feel a little unsettled.

"We'll play games!" said Amy brightly.

"Like what?"

"Oh, Musical Chairs, Pin the Tail on the Donkey . . . and we could have a piñata. Oh, *please,* Mommy? I've always wanted a piñata!" It was the first real show of enthusiasm she'd had for her party.

"Oh, honey, I don't know. . . ." My voice trailed off as I envisioned a blindfolded child wildly swinging an oversized bat within inches of the next child in line. At this point some brave soul would have to dash into the line of fire and steer the confused swinger back into piñata range. Then, when the piñata is finally broken open, and this I remember from my own childhood, there's a mad scramble to gather up the candy. And in the end very few children come away satisfied. The child who broke the piñata open doesn't get any candy because he couldn't get his blindfold off in time. The last two or three kids in line are disappointed because they never got a chance to hit it, and the rest of the party guests are bruised and bumped from their dash for goodies. "They can be kind of dangerous. We'll see," I concluded. Then, to change the subject, I said, "And I hate the elimination part of musical chairs. It never fails, the birthday girl is always the first one to get out and spends the rest of the party sulking. Pin the Tail on the Donkey is better, even though there are always a few who cheat."

"Please, can't we have a piñata?" She hadn't heard a word I'd said.

"We'll see," I repeated. "Why don't we make out the guest list and worry about party games later?"

"Okay! And can we mail the invitations today?"

"We don't even *have* the invitations yet," I answered.

"Oh! Well, let's do that, then. Let's get the invitations and the napkins and plates and all that stuff today!"

"We could do that," I answered slowly, hoping some excuse would come to mind. None did, and I felt kind of mean trying to get out of it. It would be fun to pick out the paper goods today. It takes time to get into the spirit of these things. "Looking at the party things might give us some game ideas, too," I added cheerfully. Amy beamed and I felt a flicker of party spirit. "But first the guest list," I called to her as I went to find a pencil and piece of paper. The best I could do was an envelope and a brown crayon. Oh, well, at least it wasn't yellow. "Now, who all is coming to this grand affair?"

"Oh, Mom," Amy answered, loving it. "Well, me of course," she began, and I wrote "Amy" in big letters across the top of the envelope. "And Robin and Mindy." These were neighborhood friends. I put their names below Amy's.

"What about Shannon?" I asked.

"No, she isn't really very nice. I don't want to invite her," Amy answered matter-of-factly.

"I know, but if you ask Robin and Mindy, I don't see how you can *not* ask Shannon." Shannon was a year older than Amy but Mindy's next-door neighbor, and they often all played together.

"Why not?" Amy asked.

"Well, it will hurt her feelings. Especially if we have the party here and she sees it going on." How do you explain guest-list etiquette to a five-year-old?

"Then her big sister will want to come," Amy predicted. "She came to Mindy's."

"Well, they are next-door neighbors. We'll just invite Shannon and let it go at that."

"Okay, but she'll probably come anyway."

"Well, she better not," I said more to myself than to Amy. Then, to move things along, I asked, "What about school friends?" She reeled off five or six names. "There are only ten in your class. It seems kind of mean to leave out four kids." And then, before she could suggest it, I added, "And it would make too many children to have all of them, *plus* the others. Just choose two friends from school."

"I can't. If I ask Ronnie I have to have Bobby because they're best friends. And Michelle plays with Kelly all the time, so they will want to come together. And Melissa is *my* best friend." Now it was her turn to buckle under to the status quo.

"Well, we're going to have to figure some way around all this because by the time we invite Amanda and Danny we'll be up to ten or eleven kids. I had more like six or eight in mind."

"Why do I have to ask Amanda, and *who* is Danny?"

"You invite Amanda because Maggie and I are friends and she invites you to hers. And Danny is that little boy we saw in the market the other day. I went to high school with his mom. They've just moved into the area, and he hasn't made any friends yet. I kind of mentioned your party to his mom," I explained. I knew she would accept Amanda's invitation as fair, but when I got to the part about Danny I realized I had probably overstepped my bounds.

"Oh, Mom!" She was upset with me and rightfully so. To

get myself off the hook I suggested we go then to pick out paper plates and invitations.

"If we go now we can stop for a hamburger on the way home and be back in time for naps," I said.

"Oh, boy!" Amy brightened right up and then called to her sister, "Katie! We get to have lunch at McDonald's!"

Katie looked up from her Play-Doh and asked, "Me too?"

"Yes, sweetheart, you too," I answered, giving her a squeaky kiss on her soft cheek.

I had learned about a place that specialized in party goods last year through one of the preschool moms, and we headed there now. In the car Amy announced that she was going to get rainbow plates and napkins.

"Why don't you just wait and see what's there before making up your mind?" I answered. It never failed but that when they set their hearts on something, it became impossible to find.

"Okay, but I know I want rainbows."

And, amazingly enough, they did have rainbows. Rainbows, stars, stripes, teddy bears, ducks, and rabbits; they had it all. We moved slowly down the aisle, past Strawberry Shortcake, Tom and Jerry, and Mickey Mouse, past Peter Rabbit, Star Wars, and Superman, until we came to the far wall. Then we walked up the aisle again to finalize our decision. She had narrowed it down to the rainbows or the set with the little pink kitten wearing an apron. In the end the kitten won out because you could get party bags, as well as invitations, to match.

"Oh, Mom, could we get the things for the party bags now?" Amy asked.

Well, let's see what they have."

Hanging on hooks across from the paper goods were the party favors. There were superballs and back scratchers, jacks and marbles. And I always get suckered into buying those paddles that have a ball attached to the end of an elastic band, even though I know that the band is so long that no one under four feet could begin to manage the thing. They are very popular among the fathers, though, who immediately confiscate them from the party bags and spend most of Saturday afternoon trying to beat the current record of most successive hits. Next to the paddles was the game with the numbers that slide around inside a plastic square. You know, you keep moving the numbers around in an attempt to get them in the correct numerical order. The problem with these is that they are usually so poorly made that the numbers jam and you have to resort to prying them out with a fingernail file. Other than that there were packages of plastic race cars, bracelets, corncob pipes, and animal erasers. These, however, all came in groups of six, which would mean buying two of everything. There was also a bin filled with black rubber spiders that looked kind of fun, and not to be overlooked were the brightly colored bottles of liquid bubbles with their matching magic wands, a real party-favor classic.

"Oh! Let's get some of these!" Amy called, standing on her tiptoes and trying to pull a package of honking horns off a revolving rack.

"No, those'll give me a headache bigger than the one I'm already planning on getting," I answered. "We're just going to get the plates, napkins, cups, and invitations today. If we wait, we might find some party favors we like better," I said, but by the time we headed toward the checkout counter we had added ten "fun-size" bottles of miracle bubbles and a package of balloons to our cart. I gave the spiders a last wistful look as we turned the corner.

Once at the cash register Amy was delighted to find the entire back wall covered with piñatas.

"Oh, Mom! Look at all the piñatas. . . . *Please?*" Amy's eyes were shining brightly at the colorful display. And indeed there was an assortment of shapes and sizes the likes of which I've never seen. There was a lovely green parrot with a bright orange beak, a blue guitar, a black and yellow bumble bee, a peacock with a multitude of colors, and a helicopter of red, white, and blue.

"Gosh, look at all those," I said, impressed. "They really are cute, aren't they?"

"Look, there's even a pig!" Amy pointed it out, and Katie had discovered a piñata in the shape of Big Bird.

"If we decide to have a piñata at the party we'll come back," I said firmly, but we all took one long look before going through the sliding glass doors.

We stopped at McDonald's for lunch and then hustled home for an afternoon nap. I thought I'd get a head start on the invitations while Amy was resting, but when I sat down to fill in the date, time, and place blanks, I realized that not only did I not know the day or time, we hadn't even resolved *who* was coming. Before going any further with my party plans, I decided to do some checking around.

What the Books Said

Surprisingly enough, the index of Dr. Spock's *Baby and Child Care* went from "Bibs" to "Birthmarks." I thought for sure he would have some snide remark about the trend in today's birthdays.

The Mother's Almanac recommended that "you invite no more guests than the birthday child has in years." An intriguing idea, but somehow rather impractical. But it also said that "By Five, the happiness of a party is in the weeks of anticipation, the hours of planning, with lists and invitations. . . ." Well, I was working on it. The authors went on to describe a couple of party games, but neither of them struck me as particularly great.

I like the somewhat offbeat style of *Kids: Day In and Day Out* and was pleased to see that they had devoted quite a bit of space to "Birthday Parties and Other Diversions." Two of the suggestions were for theme parties. One was an artistic party with "various collage material, playdough, easels with paint, various mediums for finger painting, and so on. The other was a party with a musical motif at which the children would "form a rhythm band to entertain the grown-ups." I had my doubts, though. If those party horns were going to be trouble, can you imagine what cymbals would do to me?

But there was also the delightful idea of going through the birthday child's baby book to remind ourselves how far we've come. I liked that a lot and made a note of it next to the ever-expanding guest list.

The other entries all pertained to older children but one dandy idea I promised myself I'd remember for a few years down the road was a County Fair party. It could be set up like the booths at a carnival, and guests would be given play money to spend at the Hot Dog (25¢), Potato Chip (5¢), or Soda (15¢) booth as well as the Ring Toss, Balloon Throw, and Photo Booth. Cute, huh?

Joan Beck's *Effective Parenting* had ten different entries under Birthday Parties. I thought I had struck it rich. "Do's and Don't's" sounded interesting, but I decided first to investigate the index subentry "for four- and five-year-olds." At first I was disappointed that the best Ms. Beck could come up with was that "Four and five year olds typically expect and want the traditional birthday party with all the classic trappings: invitations in the mail, paper streamers, party hats, cake with candles, 'Happy Birthday' singing, nut cups full of candy, balloons, favors. No additional party theme is necessary." Yet it all sounded vaguely familiar, and then I remembered why. It was precisely the kind of party Amy had asked for. It was a little unsettling, really, to think your child is so unique and then read about her in a book and realize that she is really following some predestined path to adulthood. I didn't like the idea, and to push the thought away I read on about party games. Ms. Beck suggested group treasure hunts, running games outdoors, and quiet play with crayons or pipe cleaners. I was hoping for more specific information, like *exactly* what kind of running games, but perhaps her ideas were of more help than I realized at the time. Her "Do's and Don't's" were fairly obvious ones, and here, too, was the reminder to "involve your child as much as possible in the party's planning. At least half of the fun is anticipation."

The best source I found was Louise Bates Ames and Frances L. Ilg's *Your Five Year Old.* If you're not already familiar with the handy series beginning with *Your One Year Old,* you ought to be. Chapter 8 was entirely devoted to "The Five Year Old Party" and even had a time line for the two-hour party. They recommended a planned activity that the children could work on individually while the guests (of which six was the magic number) arrived. And what do you know, pipe cleaners were once again the answer! Hmmm, maybe there was something to these pipe cleaners after all.

For the next fifteen minutes, Ames and Ilg recommended, the children should play "Game of Spider: Strings are wound around all through the house, in and out of the furniture. Each child follows her own string, winding it onto a spool. Finally each child finds a present at the end of her string." Oh, now, *that* sounded fun. I made a note of it.

Next was a clue game. Children follow from clue to clue, read out loud by the mother, until they reach the treasure, which the authors suggested be materials for a craft of some sort. Then came marching and record playing and refreshments. They never did mention opening the gifts—an easy fifteen minutes that all the kids really enjoy. Finally, they advised planning something quiet till the parents arrived to take their children home.

The "Hints and Warnings" section, not unlike Joan Beck's Do's and Don'ts, was filled with advice on expenses (keep them to a minimum), behavior (don't expect miracles), and what to do if it's an all-boy party (keep things moving). On one point, however, the authors were adamant: a "marked bag or container for their presents and favors must be provided." That, and having all the many materials ready in advance, were the biggies.

As I closed the cover of *Your Five Year Old* I noticed the small caption under the title: "Sunny and Serene," it read. Sounds good to me, I thought.

What Maggie Said

The books had helped, I'll admit, but I knew Maggie'd be able to shed some light on the situation as well. I called late that afternoon and caught her just as she was on the way out the door.

"I'm late for Ryan's ten-month checkup," she said quickly. "I'm hoping he can switch from formula to regular milk this month." Ryan had been born the previous summer, making Maggie busier than ever.

"Oh, well, you go ahead. I just need some birthday-party ideas."

"That's right! It's getting to be that time of year! I just have one word of advice—McDonald's."

"McDonald's?" I said in dismay.

"Don't act so snippy! I'll explain later. Bye-bye."

Maggie called back that evening after the kids had been tucked into bed so we could talk in peace.

"Now, what's all this about McDonald's?" I asked.

"Trust me. I did the clown for Megan's three-year-old party last January, and you were here for the magician when Amanda turned five last month, but I'll tell you, the easiest party I ever did was Amanda's four-year-old one at McDonald's."

"But that eliminates any planning on the child's part," I began.

"Yeah, I know," Maggie said, a little too enthusiastically.

"No, seriously, that's supposed to be an important part of the celebration: planning and anticipating."

"Julie, you've been reading Spock again!" Maggie teased.

"No, I haven't." I paused and then admitted, "It was *The Mother's Almanac* that said it, among others."

"I knew it!" Maggie laughed. "Hey, I'm just kidding. I agree that the birthday child enjoys the planning, but there's a lot of stress that goes along with the party. Megan cried all through the clown—"

"But—" I interrupted.

"I know, she was only three, but even Amanda at four and a half acted pretty weird. And while the magician was better, there was still all kinds of anxiety over who would be the next assistant, who couldn't see, who was bored."

"I see your point."

"It's just that when we did it at McDonald's, we walked in, sat down, opened presents, ate hamburgers, sang 'Happy Birthday,' ate the cake, and went home. Everyone had a nice time, and my house didn't look like a bomb had hit when it was all over." After a moment's hesitation, she added, "But then, with my house, who'd know the difference, right?"

We both laughed, and I said, "Oh, come on. It's not *that* bad."

"No, I guess not. And as far as Amy's party goes, you just have to do what you feel's right. But from now on, at the risk of causing my kids permanent personality disorders because their right to stuff party bags was denied them, I'm going to stick with the least stressful party arrangements possible."

"Well, you may have something there, Maggie," I said. "Listen, I've got to go. There's a great murder mystery on television in a couple of minutes and I don't want to miss the opening clues."

"Oh, that sounds good. What channel?"

"Eleven. Thanks for your help, Maggie. Now I'm *really* confused!" I joked. "Bye-bye."

But it wasn't really all that funny, and as I settled down to my movie I felt more uncertain than ever.

What My Mother Said

I knew that my mother's advice would be to keep things simple. And sure enough, when she called to see if there'd been any progress with the party plans, she reminded me, "Don't overdo, Julie. Don't try to do too much. Keep it *simple!*"

"I knew you'd say that, and believe me, I'm trying, but 'simple' isn't going to fill up a two-hour party. Maggie almost had me talked into McDonald's last night."

"Oh, Julie. I thought we agreed that those were tacky."

"Well, if you're really into simple, Maggie says—"

"Simple, yes, but you still need some individuality. Amy has already told me about the plates with the little pink kitten on them and how she wants a cake to match it."

"She does?" This was news to me.

"Yes, so you just put McDonald's right out of your head. Amy's grown up a lot this year, and she knows it. A special celebration would show her how proud of her we are. She deserves that." my mother had a way of cutting right through to the heart of the matter. I had forgotten about the undercurrent of personal success that gave this birthday its uniqueness.

"Yes, I suppose she does," I answered. "But how is that in keeping with having things simple?" Now that we were squared away philosophically, I still needed some concrete ideas to put into action.

"Why don't you go to one of those nice parks near you? That way the children could spend time playing and you'd only need a few organized games or activities."

"That's a great idea! And since the only thing Amy really feels strongly about is a piñata, maybe I'll get it after all and do that at the park." I was pleased that something had fallen into place.

"A piñata! Oh, no! I won't have it!" my mother shouted into the phone. "They're entirely too dangerous—someone is bound to get hurt. Just the thought of that big bat swinging through the air and all those small children is enough to make me sick!"

"For heaven's sake, Mom. Get a grip." I was startled by her violent attack on the piñata. "I'll talk to Jerry and see what he says. If we can't think of a safe way to do it, we just won't have one," I said to appease her.

"Well, I'm sorry, honey. I don't know what came over me, really. I never used to get so riled up over piñatas. It must be my age. When you get older, you just stop taking things for granted, I guess. Yes, you talk to Jerry. If he'll be in charge, then I guess it's okay. But I'll be the one clear across the park holding on to Katie for dear life!" We both laughed.

"Well, listen, I hear Katie crying in the bathroom, so I'd better go. She's probably flushed her underpants down the toilet. Sometimes I wish I'd never toilet-trained her—diapers did have their advantages."

"You go, honey and I'll talk to you soon."

"Bye-bye."

I hung up and went to rescue Katie, who hadn't flushed her underpants down the toilet after all—it was her socks.

What My Husband Said

There aren't many husbands who take an active role in the planning stages of a birthday party, and Jerry is no exception to the rule. He usually waits until the party paraphernalia cluttering the family room can no longer be avoided before finally asking, "So when is this party anyway?" But he's always on hand when the big day arrives to blow up balloons and race to the store for film. Come party time he greets each guest with witty remarks and snuggles down to cake and ice cream with the best of them. But since I had promised my mother I'd ask his advice about the piñata, I was going to have to draw him into the game earlier than usual.

"Amy's birthday party is a week from Saturday," I began. "Unless that isn't good for you."

"No, that sounds fine."

"I thought we'd go over to that park by the school and picnic. Amy wants a piñata. What do you think?"

"Oh, I think we can handle that. Why?"

"My mother had a fit because of the bat being so dangerous, but then she conceded that if you approved and would be in charge, she'd go along with it."

"Well, why couldn't we use Amy's plastic bat?"

"Is it heavy enough?"

"We'll take a heavier bat along just in case, but let the kids use the small one."

"Okay. But the thing *I* hate about piñatas is the pile-up when it finally breaks and all the complaints about its not being fair. I was thinking of stuffing it with individual bags with their names on them. Then there wouldn't be all that anxiety over who got the most."

"That's dumb. That takes all the fun out of it. And anyway, bags like that probably won't fall out very easily, and it'll ruin the effect of the piñata. It's not very true to life either, Julie. We don't always get our fair share wrapped up in a neat package. Kids need to learn that."

"Oh, for heaven's sake, Jerry. Our party theme is pink kittens, not 'Life is tough'!" Now I knew why I didn't ask for his help before the day of the party. But it sounded like the piñata was in. Amy would be thrilled. All I had to do now was sort through the various ideas and opinions I'd heard to arrive at the ultimate five-year-old party.

What I Did

Yes, we went to the neighborhood park, but the guests first arrived at our house so that Amy could greet them properly and have those all-important balloons on the gate. And you know, that pushy big sister of Shannon's really did come, but I sent her home. I was quite proud of myself. I'm usually not so gutsy. Amy had settled on two girls from her preschool class, and even though I stuck her with Amanda and Danny, we still had an even eight. She took cupcakes to school on Friday, and we referred to that as her "preschool party."

The children played on the swing out back until everyone

arrived, but I had purchased a few packages of colored pipe cleaners just in case of delay.

My mother had gone on ahead to the park to set up the Spider Web game. This was a big success. The gifts at the end of the yarn, bean bags, were easily hidden under bushes, under benches, or behind the drinking fountain. The strings crossed over one another in several places, so the kids really couldn't figure out where their prizes were hidden until they came to the end of the string. And it was a good thing we hadn't made the strings too long because it took a lot longer for those small hands to wind up all that yarn than we thought it would.

Jerry supervised the playground play while my mother and I set the table. We had grapes, chips, and peanut butter and jelly sandwiches. Before the children sat down to lunch I showed them where their individual party bags were so they could put their bean bags in a safe place. The magic bubbles and black rubber spiders (did you know all along I would go back for them?) were already in the bags.

The cake was a big hit. Amy had looked all through the birthday-cake notebook at Vons, but in the end decided to stick with her pink kitten. The bakery, using a napkin as a guide, had done a lovely job. Of course there were those who scraped all the frosting off and only ate the cake, as well as those who ate nothing but the sticky, sweet frosting.

And after opening gifts we played pin the tail on the donkey. Amy cheated, and her father made her take a time-out on the park bench.

Then there was the controversial piñata. Actually, Amy's enjoyment in selecting it from the store's display, as time-consuming and torturous as that was, and the fun she had in filling it with balloons, Tootsie Rolls, and plastic farm animals, probably far exceeded the fun of breaking it open.

I didn't have the nerve to stuff it with individual bags—oh, no. I didn't want to be responsible for giving these innocent children a false sense of security! Instead, I counted every balloon, Tootsie Roll, and plastic animal that went into the piñata and then figured out that each child could collect as many as eight prizes apiece. It worked great. There was still a scramble for the more popular items, but at least everyone came away with the same amount. The plastic bat didn't really have what it took to break through the piñata's stiff cardboard, but the kids had fun trying, and in the end Jerry gave it one final whack with the bigger bat while my mother and I stood half the length of a football field away with the children.

The remaining twenty minutes was free play, during which most kids played on the playground equipment, but some blew their bubbles and some ate their Tootsie Rolls. Promptly at 1:30 we piled into the cars and delivered each child to his or her doorstep. This was on the recommendation of *The Mother's Almanac* which had said, "We never met a mother who fetched her child on time, including us." And isn't that the truth? The party was a huge success. Everybody said so, but most important, Amy agreed. But it wasn't the party alone that was fun; the careful planning and sweet anticipation are what gave it that special effect we had hoped for.

Arriving home, the balloons decorating the gate were the first things I saw as I turned onto our street. One had popped, but the other three bobbed gaily in the breeze. It reminded me of something I had read somewhere. What was that? Oh, yes, I remember now, "sunny and serene." I took that as an omen and pulled into the garage humming the "Happy Birthday" tune.

5

The Trouble
with Teddy

When Katie was four she had this pink dragon that went everywhere with her. He didn't really have a name; she just referred to him as her "little guy." He was her constant companion and apparently enjoyed his exotic travels to the supermarket, car wash, bank, and library. We'd pile into the car and Katie would ask, "Where are we going again?"

"To the nursery," might be the answer.

"Oh, goody! I don't think my little guy has ever been there," she would remark cheerfully, and then proceed to explain to the pink dragon all about the nursery and tell him not to be afraid and to stay right by her so as not to get lost. The rest of us, Jerry, Amy, and I, thought it was all very cute and would exchange humorous glances and chuckle to ourselves.

Then one afternoon Katie discovered that one of her dolls' bonnets fit quite nicely on her little guy's head. It was a lovely shade of blue covered with tiny pink flowers. Once the smooth satin ribbon was tied securely under the dragon's chin (if in fact a dragon has a chin), the bonnet looked quite charming. His shiny blue eyes peeked out from under the bonnet's pink lining, the bow tied fashionably off to one side. In fact, the bonnet lent a whole new perspective to the dragon's personality. Well, clothes make the man, they say; or, in this case, the dragon. But the most obvious effect it had was in the feminine flavor it gave the dragon's appearance.

"I thought your little guy was a boy," said Amy the first time she saw the dragon wearing the bonnet.

"It is," answered Katie.

"Oh, come on!" said Amy, a scornful seven-year-old. "Boys don't wear bonnets."

"Sometimes they do," Katie answered, holding her own.

"Oh, sure. . . . Mom!" Amy figured she could nip this in the bud by calling in a higher authority.

But I was one step ahead of her. "If Katie wants her boy-dragon to wear a bonnet, that's perfectly all right. There's no rule that says only girls can wear bonnets. And it's really none of your business anyway."

"But it's so *stupid*," she responded, getting in her customary last word.

"That's enough, Amy," I answered and gave her my you-push-me-on-this-thing-and-you'll-be-sorry look.

Katie, who had been listening carefully to this dialogue, came up with what I'm sure she thought was the perfect answer. "Well, he's a boy *and* he's a girl."

"Oh, Katie!" cried Amy, exasperated. And poor Katie, who spends most of her time trying to be like her big sister, couldn't figure out why her remark had met such disapproval.

That night at dinner Katie's dragon was perched beside her, wearing its new bonnet.

"Katie, what a nice bonnet your dragon is wearing," said

Jerry. Katie beamed and gave her dragon an affectionate squeeze.

"If you ask me, it looks weird," said Amy.

"But no one asked you, did they?" I answered. Amy went back to work on her macaroni and cheese.

"Katie sure is attached to that dragon," Jerry commented. "I don't remember Amy ever doing that."

"Oh, well, when she went through that pretending stage, she did different stuff. You remember Wonder Woman, don't you?"I laughed.

"Oh, how could I ever forget Wonder Woman," Jerry groaned good-naturedly. "What? What?" Amy jumped in. "Tell me, what did I use to do?" Amy loved hearing stories like this.

"Oh, you used to pretend to be Wonder Woman and you'd have one of us call to you from another room, 'Wonder Woman! Wonder Woman! Help me!' " I explained.

"Oh, yeah, I remember." Amy nodded. "But I forget, what did I do then?"

"Oh, you'd burst through the door and say, 'What is it? I heard you calling!' and then we'd say something like, 'Oh, Wonder Woman, I'm so glad you came! A huge boulder has fallen on top of me and is crushing my legs!' Then you'd spin around crying, 'Wonder Woman!' and when the transformation was complete you'd lift the huge boulder from my limp body and heave it out the door."

"How dumb." Amy grinned sheepishly.

"Oh, you loved it. Played it all the time. And I mean *all the time*," I said, and Jerry and I laughed, thinking back to the days when we used to argue over whose turn it was to play Wonder Woman.

"No, I was saved from a meteor this morning," Jerry would say.

"But you forget, I was almost hit by a school bus less than an hour ago! So it's *your* turn," I'd argue back.

Thinking about Wonder Woman reminded me of all the other situations Amy used to love to act out. After Wonder Woman had come Peter Pan, then Star Wars, the Wizard of Oz, and finally Annie. Eventually, playing famous characters lost its excitement, and she found another game to play. She'd pretend we were an entirely different family. After visiting with Maggie and her kids, we'd come home and I'd be Maggie, Amy'd be Amanda, Katie Megan, and so on. For hours we'd use these names and say things like, "Gee, I wonder when our daddy, Tom, will be coming home from his job at the hospital," because that's what Maggie's husband did. It was always hard to snap Amy out of these fantasies, too. We'd have to wind down gradually, easing ourselves back into the real world like a coma victim regaining consciousness. And poor Katie, barely a year old, never knew what was real and what wasn't. Which may have a lot to do with who she is today!

"Kitty" was quite popular for a while. Amy'd eat cereal from a bowl on the floor, and rub up against our legs wanting to be scratched behind her ears. And this was a game even Katie could understand. But "Kitty" gave way to Doctor, Nurse, and Television Repairman, which, in my opinion, were somewhat boring.

By this time Amy was going to preschool and there was, as there is in every class, a "bad boy." His name was Kirky, and Amy took a morbid delight in playing "Kirky." I was either the innocent bystander who got pushed down or the teacher who had to reprimand "Kirky" and give him a time-out. While I didn't fully understand all the psychological aspects of the game, it made sense to me that a normal, well-behaved child might want to misbehave in play-acting just to see what it felt like.

And then there were role reversals. You know, "I'm you and you're me" stuff. This was very popular for some time, and I even thought I would have to seek professional help, when she fortunately discovered that her talents lay elsewhere and became a stage star. Yes, "We're having a show!" became a common announcement. Tickets would be passed out and audience seating arranged. Katie enjoyed the shows because she was usually allowed to twirl across the stage with a party hat on at some point. These were fun and only lasted the length of the theme song to *E.T.*

By the time I pulled myself out of my reverie, Amy and Katie had finished their dinners and were asking about ice cream.

"My little guy would like some, too, Daddy," Katie called to Jerry, who was dishing up dessert.

"Well, you'll have to share with him. We're almost out of Rocky Road," he answered. Katie sat back in her chair and, swinging her small legs, waited happily for her ice cream.

What a funny kid, I thought to myself. During those years that Amy role-played this and that, little Katie drifted in and out of the games doing her best to keep up. I anticipated that her pretend play would be very similar to Amy's when she was of that impressionable age, but we discovered in Katie a whole different approach to fantasy. It didn't take much to get her going. The Cheerios in her bowl were islands, her corn dog a spaceship. She was constantly talking to herself and at three had an imaginary friend, Gally, who lived "beyond the hills" but was a frequent visitor. She walked a fine line, our Katie. Driving along in the car, eating dinner, or taking a walk, we'd see her lips moving and a faraway look come into her eyes. "We've lost Katie," one of us would remark. We affectionately referred to these lapses as trips to "La-La Land."

It was the same way when we tried to play with the Fisher-Price setups. Amy had always conformed to the natural restrictions of the game; the children rode the yellow bus to school, and the plastic lady with the white hair was the teacher. All the people with white masks on their faces obviously went to the hospital, and Big Bird and Cookie Monster lived in the Sesame Street house. Once everything was set up, there'd be a fire at the yellow house and a rescue truck would be called, or the hospital ambulance would be summoned to the school yard, where the freckle-faced boy had fallen off the seesaw. You know, the usual routine. But when Katie joined in, the black and white dog drove the school bus, Bert and Ernie were doctors, with Oscar manning the ambulance, and the houseboat could fly. Poor Amy, with her compulsion for organization, went nuts. "You can't do it that way, Katie!" she'd cry. Amy tried to make Katie promise she'd "play it right," and because she so wanted to be included, Katie would promise—oh, yes, indeed. But once the game got under way again, Katie would forget and lift the camper into the air, crying, "Blast off to the moon!" Amy's face was a picture.

Watching Katie play made Jerry and me realize that while Amy did do a lot of pretending, it was really of a very structured nature. There were rules to be followed and a right way of doing things. But you never knew what to expect with Katie. It was genuine fantasy. Whenever we acted out the Wizard of Oz, Katie would jump into the game as Peter Pan, who had just flown in from Never-Neverland! We would just get rid of this intrusion when there would be another knock at the palace gates and E.T. would waddle into the Emerald City. In the end, we learned to adjust to her adaptations.

Amy's ice cream bowl had been licked clean (a disgusting habit) by now, but Katie was still working on hers. Actually she was "digging for gold," she explained as she burrowed around in her ice cream in search of marshmallows.

"Well, strike it rich and come get into the bath," I answered, and Amy and I went upstairs while Jerry cleared the table.

The next morning Amy was practically out the door to catch the school bus before I heard a word out of Katie.

"What is Katie doing up there?" I asked Amy, helping her on with her jacket.

"Oh, she's trying to dress that pink dragon in doll clothes," Amy answered. "Weird, huh?"

"Well, it makes sense that if it has the bonnet, it ought to have the dress too," I said.

Just then we heard a frustrated cry from upstairs—"Oh! I hate this thing! It just won't work!"—followed by deep sobs.

"Oh, dear," I said, "trouble in Paradise."

Amy laughed, "You mean La-La Land!" Amy has a sharp sense of humor. It's one of the things I like best about her. "You'd better be off, kiddo," I said, and grabbing up her lunch, she was out the door. Ahh, that left just Katie and me in the house. Jerry always left for work by six forty-five, so we never saw much of him in the mornings. I quickly climbed the stairs to see what Katie's problem was. She was sitting in the middle of her room surrounded by doll clothes of all shapes and sizes, most of them inside out.

"What are you doing?"

"Trying to dress my little guy, but his legs are down too low, so nothing fits him."

It was true. The dragon's legs were positioned under his body in such a way that he'd never fit into one of the many doll dresses strewn across the floor. "But look!" Katie said triumphantly. "This fits *Teddy* perfectly!" And that was true too. Having given up on her dragon, Katie had found an animal easier to dress. There sat her teddy bear looking quite the lady in a pink and white cotton sundress.

"Oh, she's darling!" I said, and really meant it.

Katie spent most of that morning discovering outfits for Teddy to wear. Dolls were stripped bare so that Teddy's wardrobe might be expanded. The Three Little Kittens gave up their aprons to the cause. Baby Soft Sounds lost her good winter coat, and My Friend Mandy sacrificed her jogging suit. Katie even had the nerve to raid Snoopy's and Belle's wardrobe case in Amy's room. And if it didn't fit Teddy, she found some other stuffed animal who wore that size. By eleven o'clock, she had outfitted everything from lambs and bunny rabbits to elephants and owls. It was something to behold, all right. At least I was impressed. And so was Amy when she arrived home from school that afternoon. In fact, after we resolved a minor skirmish over the Snoopy clothes, Amy decided to dress a few stuffed animals of her own.

Because most of the clothes fit him the best, Katie's teddy bear became her all-time favorite. The pink dragon stepped down, faithful friend that he was, to allow Teddy a place in the sun.

"Oh, don't worry, Mommy," Katie assured me when I expressed a concern that her little guy might have its feelings hurt. "He's baby-sitting that whole gang in my room. I put him in charge, and he reads to them and makes sure everyone gets to bed on time." It still sounded like a cut in rank to me. I'd much rather loll back in a baby buggy or ride perched on a bicycle basket than read books to that bunch of weirdos up in Katie's room. But who am I to judge?

Then she started misplacing Teddy. He was constantly being left face down on the bathroom counter or staring up at Katie's dresses from the closet floor. This, on its own, was not unusual. Katie was notorious for forgetting where she left her shoes or for leaving her purse behind in restaurants. I'd send her upstairs to get a jacket and then come across her later building a Lego space station, having completely forgotten her original errand. Helium balloons were never long for this world when in Katie's charge. It all had something to do with La-La Land, I think. So Teddy's temporary abandonments did not surprise any of us. It was Katie's violent reaction the moment she realized Teddy was missing that was so uncharacteristic. Under ordinary circumstances she was the last to know if something had been forgotten. So her panicked cry of "My Teddy! Wait! Where is Teddy?" should have clued us in that she was getting in over her head. But it didn't. It was a remark from a neighbor that caused me to take a closer look at Katie's behavior. Katie was riding her bicycle along the sidewalk out in front of our house when the dip of a driveway caused her bike to tip unsteadily on its training wheels. Teddy, who had been squeezed into the basket, tumbled out. Katie's cries of anguish brought not only me running but several other neighbors who had been watching their children at play. We all assumed Katie had hurt herself the way she was carrying on, but there she was, still seated upon her bike!

"Katie! What on earth is wrong?" I demanded when I arrived at the scene. A child's own mother is the least sympathetic.

"Teddy, Teddy!" she wailed. "Teddy fell out!"

"Oh, for God's sake, Katie! You scared us half to death." I picked Teddy up and, brushing him off roughly, stuffed him back into her basket.

"Don't! You're hurting him," Katie pleaded. "Let me see him." I handed him to her, disgusted. My heart was still pounding from the scare she had given me.

"She sure has gone off the deep end about that bear," remarked my neighbor.

"Yeah, I know," I answered. "But I think it's hard to be

the youngest. Teddy's her own little buddy and something Amy doesn't have." I tried to sound convincing, not just for my neighbor but for myself as well. I hadn't really noticed until this afternoon how attached to him she was.

That evening I asked Jerry if he thought Katie was too "wrapped up" in her bear.

"Oh, I don't know. Why?"

I told him about the incident with the bike.

"Well, it could be that she's placing too much significance on Teddy. Relying on him too much, so to speak. I'll talk to her about it tonight." Oh, this should be interesting.

So just before bedtime Jerry called Katie over to him. "Katie, I want to talk to you about your teddy bear."

"Teddy! Where is he?" Her eyes looked a bit wild and her voice sounded frightened, if not frantic. I wondered if Jerry noticed.

"He's right *here*," answered Amy, tossing Teddy, who had just slipped off the coffee table, to her sister. Katie retrieved Teddy, smoothed out his dress, and settled him comfortably in her lap. When she looked up at Jerry expectantly, her eyes were clear and bright. Maybe I was imagining things.

"What, Daddy?"

"I think it's nice that you have a teddy bear that you love so much, and I like how you take such good care of him. It's almost like he's a real friend, isn't it?" Jerry began.

"Uh-huh," Katie agreed. She was retying the bow on his apron.

"But you need to remember that Teddy's only a stuffed bear. He's not a real bear," Jerry came right to the point.

"Sometimes he's real." The bow still wasn't right and she began again.

"Only in your imagination, honey," Jerry said a little smugly, figuring he'd gotten around that one. But I knew better. Katie would interpret that as an admission that there was, in fact, a time and place for Teddy to be real. Now it was her turn to smile smugly. "Do you understand, Katie?"

"Uh-huh. Could you tie the bow on his apron, Daddy? It's too hard for me."

"Sure, honey," he answered, and then flashed me a kind of quizzical look that seemed to ask, "What do you think?"

That was on a Tuesday, and by the time the weekend rolled around things hadn't changed. In fact, if anything, they were worse. Teddy not only went everywhere with Katie, he had to be dressed appropriately, too. To preschool he wore his pink overalls, to tumbling class an old bathing suit of Katie's modified to look like a leotard, and always to bed his blue pajamas (contraband from Snoopy's closet). Once, when we set out for storytime at the library, Katie completely fell apart because Teddy was still in his pajamas. She was so distraught over the whole thing that I turned the car around halfway to the library so that Teddy could quicky change into his sundress. It was probably a stupid thing to do, and I wondered later how much irrevocable damage I had done. But it seemed so important to her, and what difference did it make to me? It was *her* storytime. I didn't want to send her into the library in tears! And I almost had myself convinced that it was okay . . . almost, but not quite.

And so, when Jerry offered to take the girls for a bike ride around the neighborhood Saturday morning, I made sure Katie was forewarned to dress herself *and Teddy* for the occasion. But even so, a scene could not be avoided. It was colder outside than Jerry had anticipated, so he sent Amy and Katie back into the house for sweatshirts. They dashed in and then back out again, anxious to be on their way. What happened next isn't hard to guess. Realizing that Teddy didn't have on *his* sweater, Katie called to Amy and Jerry to wait while she went to get it. Knowing only too well that sending Katie for Teddy's sweater could take anywhere from five to fifteen minutes, they both agreed that Teddy should just ride in what he had on.

"Katie, he's fine. A T-shirt is enough for a bear. He's got fur," reasoned Jerry.

"Yeah, c'mon, Katie. Teddy likes the cold," added Amy.

But Katie wouldn't hear of it. "He needs his sweater." Her voice shook.

"Katie, Amy and I are leaving for our bike ride now. We are not waiting while you rummage around looking for that bear's sweater. Are you coming or not?"

Having followed the girls back outside after their sweatshirt run, I was witness to the scenario. When both Amy and Jerry started in on Katie about her bear, I came very close to defending her. But I interfere too much as it is and I've got to learn to let them work things out without me. Even so, I was on the verge of racing upstairs and frantically searching for Teddy's sweater myself when Jerry's tone of voice changed my mind. We have always tried not to contradict each other in front of the children, and I knew from the set of his jaw and the coolness of his voice that he wanted control of this situation.

"But, Daddy . . . " Katie began. She was trying hard not to cry.

"We'll ride around for a few minutes and then check back to see if you're ready," Jerry interrupted her. But his voice had softened at her pathetic attempts to control her tears. He and Amy rode off, and Katie broke down and sobbed. Oh, how my heart ached for her. Now I was the one fighting for control.

"Katie," I said softly. "Come here, sweetheart." Noticing me for the first time, she ran into my arms and clung to my neck, crying bitterly, "They wouldn't wait! They wouldn't wait for me!"

Knowing I had to support Jerry's decision to leave her

behind, I answered, "No, honey, it was Teddy they wouldn't wait for. If it had been *your* sweatshirt, they would have waited, but they didn't want to wait for a *bear*—a bear who really doesn't know if it's cold or not."

Katie looked at me, a little surprised. Tears still clung to her eyelashes and streaked down her cheeks. "What do you mean?" she asked.

"Well, he's not *real*, Katie. He can't feel the cold. He *is* just a stuffed animal." Katie's eyes drifted over to where Teddy was perched in her bike basket. His glass eyes gazed off into the distance. When she looked back up into my face she said simply, "They should have waited for me," and started crying again. As I held her small, sobbing body, I realized that I didn't know whether to play into her fantasy or keep both her feet firmly planted on the ground. I loved Katie's spontaneous imagination and had no intention of putting a permanent damper on it, but she seemed to be in trouble with Teddy.

"Come on. Dry your eyes, blow your nose, and let's go get Teddy's sweater so you'll be ready when they come back by," I suggested.

By the time Jerry and Amy sped around the corner, Katie had pulled herself together and was all set to go.

"All ready, Katie?" Jerry called cheerfully.

"Uh-huh," Katie answered, still a little subdued.

"Okay, you lead the way," and then to me he said, "I know you think it was mean of us to leave without her—"

"Broke her heart is all," I interrupted.

"But we have to stop making allowances for her all the time. If she's going to continue this teddy-bear thing, then she'll have to learn to accept the consequences." Jerry has always been big on consequences. "If you think of a better way to handle the situation, let me know," he concluded and then followed the girls down the street.

Yeah, well, any suggestion from me would be like the

blind leading the blind at this point. A little research was in order here; research and perhaps a few encouraging words to put the problem into perspective.

What the Books Said

When I was at the library for Katie's storytime, I picked up a copy of *Ask Dr. Salk* but hadn't taken the time to look through it yet. Now was the time. The book is composed entirely of questions from parents. Like case histories, these kinds of books can be very revealing and often make me realize how lucky I am not to have the other person's problem. I read all about the poor woman whose teenager is always late and another one whose in-laws constantly talk baby talk to their four-year-old son before I got to the section on imaginary playmates. A mother, concerned because her five-year-old boy was blaming an imaginary friend for a lot of things that he was actually doing himself, had written Dr. Salk for advice. At first I was disappointed—resolving problems through fantasy play wasn't really what I was after—but Dr. Salk did say that while an imaginary playmate is not harmful, the child should be aware that it *is* make-believe. I thought about how Katie had looked at Teddy in the bike basket the other day. Surely she didn't *really* think he was real. I read on, "It is important for children to be able to make the distinction between what is real and what is pretend. Some parents are afraid that they will rob a child of the pleasure of play by making this clear, but their fears are unfounded. Children can relate quite vividly and emotionally to make-believe events, and this gives them great latitude for the expression of their ideas and feelings." This helped to clarify the question of whether or not to feed into Katie's fantasy. I guess I did need to keep her more aware of reality. Dr. Salk then addressed himself to the original question and advised that the parents make sure their son knows that he alone is responsible for the imaginary playmate and will have to pay the consequences of his wrongdoings. Hmmm, sounded like something Jerry would say. There was some further discussion of predictions and expectations before the next letter, concerning hero worhip, was answered. Afraid of getting sidetracked by "The Biting Toddler" or "Beauty Contests for Children," I closed *Ask Dr. Salk* and scanned the shelf for another likely reference.

"Imagination" fell between "Illness" and "Impetigo" in the index to Spock's *Baby and Child Care*. The fact that ony two pages were listed was not very encouraging; Katie's was more a three- or four-page problem, I figured. But I was mistaken. Right after stating that a little imagination is a good thing, he said, "On the other hand, if he's spending a good part of each day telling about imaginary friends or adventures, not as a game but as if he believes in them, it raises the question whether his real life is satisfying enough." Satisfying? Katie's life wasn't *satisfying?* Well, how was that supposed to make me feel? God, now I was really depressed. Then he mentioned that the child should have friends his own age to play with. No problem there. Katie had several neighborhood friends she played with daily. As I forced myself to read on, he continued, "Another question is whether he is having enough easy going companionship with parents. A child needs hugging and piggyback rides. He needs to share in his parents' jokes and friendly conversations. If the adults around him are undemonstrative, he dreams of comfy, understanding playmates as the hungry man dreams of chocolate bars." Hugging! Piggyback rides! Why, that's what we do best! Friendly conversation? Ours are the friendliest conversations you'll ever hear! Jokes? He wants jokes? Did you hear what the mother said to the psychologist? . . . I'll give him jokes. Oh, Spock, you're way off base on this one. That's what I hate about reading these child-care books. Most of these professionals don't *really* know what's going on. Their advice isn't based on your own personal experience but on some general trend. But because it is written in a book by someone with a list of degrees after his name, it has the power to shake, if not shatter, your own self-confidence. In my particular situation I thought Dr. Spock was wrong; he didn't have all the facts to make the judgment he did. But still, the suggestion that Katie's real life wasn't satisfying haunted me.

From "Curiosity and Imagination" Spock went into "Fears'" of the dark, dogs, and death. Not wanting to borrow trouble and having heard enough, thank you, I replaced *Baby and Child Care* on the bookshelf.

I glanced through the indexes of several other books, and once, in scanning the page for "Imagination," my eyes caught the entry "Insanity, rarity of." I paused just long enough to consider that if it's all that rare, I won't worry about insanity. Actually, "Imagination" or "Imaginary play" was a lot more difficult to find than I'd thought it would be. "Image-making" went right into "Imitation, learning by," and in one case "I Met a Penguin" followed "I Love Lucy." I tried looking under "Pretend," but there was usually a jump from "Preschoolers" to "Prickly heat." I gave up and went to see what unsatisfying activity Katie was engaged in.

What Maggie Said

Maggie and I had arranged to meet at a park on Monday for a picnic lunch with the kids. The older girls were in school now, and Katie and Megan attended preschool on different days. Our weekly visits with Maggie and her girls had been drastically reduced. But Monday was a school holiday, and we decided to take advantage of it.

The weather was beautiful, and Amy helped me make the peanut butter and jelly sandwiches while Katie got Teddy ready for the day's outing.

"I'll probably have to hold him most of the time," Katie remarked. "He doesn't really know those other kids, and he might cry if I put him down."

Amy rolled her eyes at me.

"Well, you just be sure you have everything you need because we are *not* coming back for anything," I said firmly.

"I know!" she answered cheerfully. "I packed everything in his backpack."

Once we got to the park the kids scattered. Amy and Amanda climbed to the top of the rocket ship, shouting orders back and forth to blast off, Megan headed for the slide, little Ryan began pushing his trucks through the deep drifts of sand, and Katie, having strapped Teddy into the baby swing, was pushing him gently.

"She does a lot of that, doesn't she?" remarked Maggie. She was looking over in Katie's direction. Following her gaze, I could see Katie's lips moving as she chatted happily to Teddy. She was in a world of her own.

"Yeah, she does," I answered thoughtfully. "In fact, I'm a little worried she does it too much."

"What do you mean?" Maggie asked.

"Well, this whole thing with the teddy bear. They're inseparable; she plays with it all the time, and I'm beginning to wonder if she doesn't believe it's real. Now, how crazy does *that* sound?" I laughed, trying to sound casual, but I knew Maggie saw through my act, as I had hoped she would.

"Does she take the bear to preschool?"

"Well, she took him once to 'share,' and then after that I made her leave him in the car."

"And was that a problem?"

"It was touch-and-go there last Friday. She wouldn't get out of the car without him, and I was just about to give in when I remembered that her class was walking to the supermarket, so I told her bears weren't allowed to go and that Teddy would be happier with me than left alone in the classroom. I got away with it, but I doubt if I will again," I answered. Then, to give her some further background, I told her about the bike-ride episode as well as what I had read in Dr. Spock.

"Oh, for heaven's sake, Julie! I hope you didn't take him too seriously!" Maggie said, referring to Spock's remark about unsatisfying lives.

"Well, I didn't at first . . . but the more I think about it . . ."

"Oh, come on, it's just her 'thing' right now. Remember Amy and all that crazy role-playing she used to do? And what about when Amanda was that dog and crawled around licking everyone's ankles? God, it was disgusting, but she got over it. They're just exercising their imaginations."

"You think so?" I asked hopefully.

"Absolutely. And as far as that teddy bear goes, why don't you have her switch to a new animal every so often? Maybe that way, too strong an attachment to any one animal will be avoided," Maggie advised.

"That's a good idea." I felt quite encouraged. "Her room is filled with furry creatures all dressed up with no place to go. I'll suggest that they take turns."

The kids started to beg for lunch, so Maggie and I began the ritual of unscrewing thermos tops, pulling open Frito bags, and starting banana peels. I felt so much better after talking to Maggie that I didn't bat an eye when Katie spread her napkin out in front of Teddy and proceeded to arrange bits of sandwich on it. The kids soon returned to their play, and Maggie and I sat contentedly in the warm sun munching on leftover bread crusts and discussing Maggie's new job selling potted plants through home parties.

What My Mother Said

That afternoon my mother stopped by to return Jerry's power saw my dad had used over the weekend.

"It was just an excuse to come by and give Amy and Katie a quick squeeze," she said in response to my comment that there was no hurry for the saw.

Amy and Katie had been playing on the swing set out in back when my mother arrived and, after Amy demonstrated her latest daredevil trick on the trapeze bar, Katie showed how Teddy could swing upside down by his knees.

"Oh! Katie! You're scaring me!" my mother feigned horror at the dangerous exhibition.

"Don't worry, Grandma. He won't fall," she answered, pleased with the response Teddy's trick had induced.

I backed my mother away from the swing set and said quietly, "Don't feed into this Teddy thing too much, Mom."

"Why? What's wrong?"

"Well, Jerry and I just think she's gone a little overboard on the whole thing. She goes into a complete state of panic if she misplaces him. He's become her whole life, it seems like."

My mother turned to the swing set and watched Katie help Teddy climb the ladder up to the slide. "Oh, I don't know, Julie. I don't think you should take that away from her. Teddy makes her happy, fills a void that needs filling right now. I can't see that it can possibly do any harm."

"You don't think she really *believes* her teddy bear's alive, do you?" I asked because that was, after all, the real issue.

"Is that what's worrying you? No, I don't. Look how attached she was to that funny pink dragon, but then she dropped him like a shot because the doll clothes fit Teddy better."

"Yeah, that's true. It's just that it's hard to pin her down about it. Jerry talked to her about Teddy not being real, but she just kept changing the subject."

"Well, of course she did," my mother answered. "She doesn't want to admit he's a stuffed bear. It would ruin her game. Julie, she's the littlest one in the family, she doesn't have anyone younger to either boss around or take care of. Everybody walks faster, talks faster and knows more. She can't possibly keep up so she's created her own world in which she's the one in charge."

"Except that she's not . . ." I started.

"Oh, yes she is," my mother interrupted. "She knows just what she's doing. I think it would be cruel of you to take it away from her."

I didn't answer right away and we stood in silence watching the girls play happily and listening to their sweet voices ring out in the late afternoon.

"So you think she's okay?" I asked again, just for verification.

"I think she's extraordinary. You know that. And I think you and Jerry ought to leave her alone. Or if you do anything, be more patient with her, give her a little more time. A little extra love."

I thought about Dr. Spock and "easy going companionship" and wondered if perhaps we weren't as easy going as we thought we were.

I sighed and my mother looked over at me. "I'm not being critical, you know that. But you *did* ask my opinion."

"I know," I answered. "And it helps, it really does."

What My Husband Said

Hanging up the phone, I announced, "That was your mother."

"Oh?" Jerry had just settled down to a James Bond movie on television.

"Why didn't you tell me that Katie had your mom fix Teddy his own lunch this weekend?" I asked accusingly. Helen had invited them all over for lunch on Sunday.

But instead of answering, Jerry hushed me with a wave of his hand.

"Oh, this is great. Watch." He pointed to the television screen. I looked over just in time to see James Bond ski wildly down a mountain, several Russian agents hot on his trail, then sail dramatically off a sheer cliff, only to be rescued at the last minute by a cleverly disguised parachute. At this point Carly Simon broke into the theme song.

"Can I continue now, or do you want me to remain standing until the song is over, like the national anthem?"

"Oh, I'm sorry. I didn't mean to interrupt you. I just thought you'd want to see that part; it's a great scene. Go ahead, there's a commercial on now."

The term "crime of passion" probably found its origin in just such a conversation. But since I didn't think it would hold up in a court of law, I simply repeated the question.

"Oh, yeah," Jerry recalled. "Teddy's lunch. He had peanut butter and honey. Get it? Honey, for a bear?" I could tell from his sappy smile that he thought it was cute.

"Honestly, Jerry, you're worse than she is! Here I am trying to resolve this whole bear issue and you're making jokes!"

He looked up at me in surprise, "Are you really that worried about her?"

"Yes." I filled him in on what Dr. Spock and Dr. Salk had to say as well as Maggie and my mother.

"Well, your mother babies Katie too much, and Maggie's idea of changing animals is okay, but it just kind of muddies the water as opposed to dealing directly with the problem. As far as Spock goes, I just don't buy that we aren't loving or satisfying enough for Katie. That other guy, Salk, seems to be more to the point." See, I knew he'd go for that bit about consequences. "But the truth of the matter is, Julie, I think you're making a mountain out of a molehill."

"How can you say that? You saw how she fell apart the other day before the bike ride!"

"Well, I just think it's a stage and it'll pass. In the meantime let's all try to be more considerate of her needs. Okay?"

"Okay. . . ." I really wasn't quite through with the subject, but I could see he was. His show was back on and receiving his full attention. Any further attempt to discuss the matter on my part would be futile. I resigned myself to an evening with 007 and picked up the story just as James leaped onto the hood of some gorgeous blonde's car.

What I Did

I decided to try Maggie's approach first and use it as a kind of test. If Katie couldn't change bears just for a day, I'd take to serious worrying. But after some initial hesitation Katie decided she liked the idea and even lined her animals up in the order in which they'd have their turn. We took to calling it "friend-for-a-day." This turn of events gave me considerable relief.

But because it haunted me that perhaps Katie turned to her stuffed playmates because her real world was too tense, I took special care to gear activities, stories, and even conversations (the friendlier the better) down more to her level. With the more relaxed atmosphere Katie herself became more easygoing and less prone to hysterics when a bear became misplaced or left behind. She still talked to her waffles, though. And Lego villagers continued to invade Tub Town from the air, but I wouldn't have wanted it any other way.

6

The Extracurricular Experiment

"Mom! I'm home!"

That would be Amy, home from school. I still couldn't get used to the idea of her being in first grade. Kindergarten was a milestone, to be sure, but only three hours long; Amy was practically home before Katie was dressed! And you know how it is with kindergarten—they're kind of a separate entity in the school as it is. But first grade was the real thing. It was individual desks as opposed to group tables. Yes, that says it all—a desk implies responsibility, independence, a home away from home. Oh, it was going to be a great year, full of new experiences and new friends.

"I'm in here!" I called to Amy from the bedroom, where I was folding laundry. Amy came into the room, grinning happily, flung down her book bag, and flopped onto the bed. Several neat stacks of folded clothes toppled over in her direction.

"Don't jounce the clean clothes, honey," I remarked automatically. "So how was school today?"

"Perfect!" she answered cheerfully. And to think that this was the same child who spent an entire year of preschool clinging to my leg. All that would have been a lot less painful if I could have looked ahead to this cozy bedroom scene. But, hey, that would have made things too easy.

The contents of Amy's bag had spilled out onto the floor, exposing an assortment of fliers, notices, and other important communiques between school and home. Having folded the last T-shirt and paired up the last sock (well, yes, there did seem to be one odd sock left over, another sacrifice to the laundry god having been made), I gathered up the papers and began to take a closer look. There was a notice announcing a change in the bus schedule, a card to be returned verifying immunizations, a school menu, a friendly welcome from the school principal, and, under the PTA message to all new parents, the after-school program sign-up sheet.

"Look at this, Amy," I said, studying the flier with interest. "They have Kid Cookery on Tuesday afternoons and Dinosaur Days on Thursdays."

"No, that doesn't sound that great. Anyway, I'm already taking gymnastics." She was always so sensible, just like her father. God, they were irritating.

"Well, that's on Mondays. The rest of the week is free. . . . Look, here's a drawing class—you love to draw, don't you?"

"Yeah, but—"

"Just let me read what's available and you tell me if anything sounds interesting. You don't *have* to take a class, but I think you'd enjoy taking something like this." I began to reel off all the different classes being offered. There were classes in karate, music, Spanish and math (actually entitled

MathaMagic, as if that were going to fool anyone into thinking that it was more fun than facts), as well as space travel, water painting, beginning computers, and reading (formally called Reading Rainbow—only a kindergartner would be tricked by that one). Kitchen Chemistry and Clay Play were the only two that caught Amy's interest. Clay Play, however, was on Mondays from two forty-five to three forty-five.

"That's okay, I'll just do the chemistry one, then. What is chemistry anyway?" Amy asked.

"Oh, I think you probably do experiments with different ingredients found in the everyday kitchen. But listen, back to Clay Play, if I picked you up at the bus stop and you changed into your leotard in the car, you could still make it to gymnastics on time."

"I guess." She sounded doubtful.

"Now, Kitchen Chemistry is on Thursdays, but it's held over in the recreation building. You'd just have time for an after-school snack before I drove you over there."

"That's okay. I want to do that one. The clay class makes too much happening in one day." There it was again, the voice of reason.

"Fine. Kitchen Chemistry it is." I filled out the registration card and put it, along with a check, into an envelope. Slipping the envelope into her school bag, I felt a surge of accomplishment. Yes, I was organizing activities for my first-grader quite nicely.

Later that day I received a phone call from a neighbor friend who wanted to know if Amy was going to be a Brownie Scout this year.

"Gee, I don't know. I didn't think they did that in first grade. When I was a girl, Brownies started in second," I answered.

"Yes, well they've come up with this new policy so that all

the good kids and potential leaders don't jump the gun and go with Bluebirds."

"What?" I asked, unable to follow this logic.

"It's really quite simple, Julie. Because the Bluebird program begins in the first grade, moms who can't wait for their daughters to begin something, *anything,* sign up for the Bluebirds, and then in the second grade, when it's time to set up Brownie troops, all these overachievers, who make great leaders, have already been scooped up. Don't you see?" she said, and then continued, "Now, the Girl Scout Council will tell you they've expanded their program to meet a rising demand or something like that, but don't you believe it. It was primarily designed to get the girls before someone else did," she concluded confidently.

"Well, that makes sense, I guess. I didn't realize that our kids were in such demand!" I joked weakly.

"Oh, Julie, you're so naive. Haven't the soccer people called you yet?"

"No. . ." I trailed off. I didn't think I wanted to hear about "the soccer people." They sounded ominous, sort of like "the body snatchers."

"Oh, well, they will. That's a real pushy group. You'll be team mom before you even know what hit you," she warned me. Yes, it definitely smacked of a conspiracy.

"This all sounds a little overwhelming," I confessed. "Amy has a gymnastics class on Mondays, and I just signed her up for an after-school chemistry class on Thursdays. I think that about covers things. I mean, they do have *school,* you know. And first grade is a tough year." I tried to sound firm, but I knew in my heart how weak I really was. I'm a sucker for anxiety, and just the thought that I might miss the boat with Brownies and Amy would wind up in a second-rate troop next year made my palms sweat. "Listen, let me talk to Amy about this Brownie thing and I'll get back to you later." I wanted to draw the conversation to a close before anything else came up.

"Well, you'd better let me know by the end of the week. I'm turning in my troop list Friday."

My hands went sticky again. "Well, why don't you just go ahead and put her down. I'm sure she'll want to do it. If there's any problem, I'll let you know before the weekend." I hung up feeling disgusted with myself, but at least my hands were beginning to dry out.

Amy was thrilled with the idea of Brownies. "And Mom, you get to wear special outfits with orange tassles on the socks. Kathy's a Brownie, she's got them." Oh, well, that cinched it. If Kathy was doing it, we must be on the right track. Kathy lived across the street. She was only a year older than Amy but had savvy well beyond her years. She was everything Amy ever hoped to be. So the fact that Kathy wore the plain brown jumper and funny little beanie with her usual cool confidence gave the whole organization some class. And Amy was in. Whew! That was a close one. So this would work out: Mondays to gymnastics for health and fitness, Tuesdays would be Brownies for social skills and service to one's community, and then Thursday's Kitchen Chemistry class would round out the week with a little intellectual stimulation. It was the perfect program.

When the phone rang the next day I almost didn't answer it. I had the J. C. Penney's catalogue open in front of me and was making a list of all Amy's Brownie needs. Figuring it was better to be safe than sorry, I had decided to phone in my order that day lest they run out of "flashes," as the orange sock tassles were called, in the September rush. But I did answer, an act I would soon regret. It was someone named Donna from the community soccer commission. My heart sank. I wasn't up to this. I could tell from her opening remarks that I was no match for Donna.

"I got your name from a friend who said you might be

interested in coaching one of our first-grade soccer teams," Donna said, coming right to the point.

"Oh, really? Who was that?" I racked my brain trying to think of which "friend" would play such a rotten trick. I vowed revenge.

"Oh, gee, I don't seem to have that information in front of me just now, but we sure could use your help. Your daughter *is* playing soccer this year, isn't she?"

Oh, but they were a smooth bunch. I thought back to my conversation with the Brownie lady. Yes, she had predicted this very thing. "Well, actually, no, she isn't. She—" but before I could explain, Donna interrupted me.

"Oh, no, really? Gosh, the kids have such a good time, and it's all very low key. Games are on Saturdays, with half an hour's practice just before each game. There's no obligation during the week. It's a special time for the whole family to come and cheer the kids on."

Oh, that was tricky. In other words, not signing up for soccer is like not loving your family. I wondered if being a good American would figure into the conversation.

"And you know, the children who play in these younger grades are able to build upon the positive experience and become more competent and better team players later on," she continued. Well, what could be more American than being a team player? And at the same time she hinted at the fact that my child would be *behind* if she decided to play soccer in, say, fourth grade. Ooh, that was almost as clever as the Brownie leader letting me believe Amy would not be in the "right" troop. This was getting awfully complicated! Beads of sweat began to collect on the palms of my hands.

"Well," I began uncertainly, but then, afraid Donna would hear the hesitation in my voice, I said quickly, "She really has too many other activities right now. Maybe next year."

But it was too late. Donna sensed my insecurity, and

having found the crack in my armor, she persisted until there was nothing left for me to do but give in (Are you horribly disappointed in me?) But I would *not* be team mom. On that issue I held firm . . . opting for refreshments instead. Hanging up the phone, I admitted to myself that I had been unequivocably duped, my body snatched in broad daylight.

When Amy came home from school that day, she was dubious about this latest commitment.

"Mom, I really think it's too much," she said calmly, shaking her head.

"I know, I blew it, but this lady talked me into it. It's only Saturdays, and we'll all go as a family. Actually you might be glad later that you had this experience. I mean if you play when you're older."

She gave me a long, hard look, uncertain whether or not to believe that I went along with that. "It's okay, Mom," she said patting me on the back. "It'll probably be fun."

"Oh, thank you," I answered, relieved. Thanking her for what, I don't know . . . understanding, I guess.

It didn't happen all at once. No, it was a classic case of snowballing, one event piling up after another. Kitchen Chemistry started first, and then two weeks later Brownies began their Tuesday meetings. And soccer got off to an innocent start—until her team ended in the playoffs. Her coach, dazzled by the possibility of a championship team (who cares if they're only in first grade?), began scheduling practices during the week. This was about the same time that the Brownies decided to set up a booth at the local Octoberfest. This event would require a simple costume (how hard could it be to make a felt vest?) and an extra afternoon meeting to practice a German folk dance. I should have caught on at this point, but I didn't. It wasn't until I read the gymnastics monthly newsletter that I began to feel a little uncomfortable. There was to be a ten-year anniversary celebration in two weeks. The phrase "student demonstrations" jumped out at me, and I scanned the page for the word "costume." It wasn't there, but "rehearsal," almost as bad, was. Getting out my calendar, I began pinpointing the various rehearsal dates. Well, she'd be a few minutes late but could make it to Thursday's. Friday looked okay, but I seemed to remember something about soccer being changed from Wednesday, and when was that Brownie dance practice? While I was collecting the various notices off the refrigerator door, Amy's big orange pumpkin announcing the school Halloween carnival slid to the floor. Oh, yeah, that was coming up too.

It must have been as I was squeezing times and places into the two-inch squares of my calendar that I began to realize the absurdity of it all. I was able, however, to divert these foreboding thoughts by telling myself that *everyone* has a busy schedule. But once the week got under way, I could fool myself no longer. We had definitely overdone. And I say "we" not only because I recognize my role in getting us into this mess in the first place, but because when you live with an overinvolved child, the entire family suffers. For example, on Mondays a neighbor baby-sits Katie until 1:30 while I am at work. Katie and I arrive home just before Amy, who gets out of school at 1:45, and then there's usually just enough time for a short rest for Katie, some quiet time for me and Amy, and then a snack for both girls before Amy and I are off to gymnastics. On this particular Monday, however, there was a 2:45 rehearsal scheduled, so we had to skip quiet time and Katie, the world's slowest eater, brought her snack along in the car. Once we'd delivered Amy to her class, Katie and I headed over to the mall in search of green felt for the Octoberfest costume.

"Can I stay in the car?" Katie asked as I pulled into a parking spot. She was still working on her granola bar.

"No, honey. You kow how I feel about that." I had once left Amy and Katie in the car while I ran into the post office, and when I had returned to the car both girls were gone. I stared in disbelief at the empty seats and felt my entire body grow cold. I thought of fainting. At least it would be an escape from the nightmare, but the resounding thought "Jerry will kill me" kept me alert. Only a split second had actually elapsed, and just as I was about to scream, for I had decided that screaming was the next best thing to fainting, the blanket in the far back of the car was tossed aside, revealing Amy and Katie, triumphant in having pulled off the trick. I never left them alone in the car again. Seeing their wide grins and hearing their gay laughter after being sure they were lost felt like a mircale to me. I took it as a sign, a warning, and have never allowed myself to forget the horror of that split second. The girls, of course, thought it was hysterical and couldn't wait to tell Dad. What made them think he would see the humor of the joke was beyond me. But they never failed to report these offbeat stories, which usually left me with some explaining to do.

So Katie staggered along beside me while we made our purchases, and by the time I'd stopped for gas and made a speed run into the market for milk, it was time to pick Amy up.

While I got dinner ready, Amy did her spelling homework and Katie watched the last half-hour of *Sesame Street*. Twice I heard her let out a heavy sigh. The poor kid was tired. And sure enough, she fell asleep at the dinner table, her head resting on her chest, her spoon still full of mashed potatoes.

"What happened to Katie?" Jerry asked.

"Oh, she just had a really busy day," I answered.

Tuesday it rained. Katie went to preschool, and I was through with my last "Mommy and Me" tumbling class in time to pick her up from school. I was determined to give her a nap today, and she did rest quietly for a while before Amy burst through the kitchen door. She was soaking wet.

"How did you get so wet?" I asked.

"It's raining." Ask a stupid question . . .

"I *know* it's raining, but you have an umbrella. Didn't you use it?

"I shared with Missy. She forgot hers," she answered and then brightened up considerably and asked, "We want to put our boots on and play in the gutter. She's asking her mom. Can I?"

"For a little while, but you've got Brownies this afternoon."

"Oh, yeah. It seems like there's something every day. When is there a day I can just play?"

But the phone rang and I didn't have to answer her. Good thing, too, because I don't know what I would have said. Anticipating Missy's call, Amy had picked up the phone.

"Oh. I can't either. I've got Brownies," Amy was saying. There was a pause, and Missy must have said something funny because Amy laughed and then said, "Okay, see you tomorrow. 'Bye." She hung up the phone and said, "She's got piano lessons today."

"Oh?" I said, and I must have sounded interested because Amy gave me a steady look and said firmly, "*I* don't want to take piano lessons," and then she added, "Anyway, Missy says they're boring."

Amy's Brownie meetings lasted an hour. I usually took Katie to a nearby park where we played until the meeting was over. But it continued to rain, so instead Katie and I sat in the car. I attempted to read to her, but she wanted to "play house." So while she adjusted the seats up and down and arranged a bed in the back of the car, I reclined my seat, closed my eyes and pretended to be "the mom who sleeps a lot." I didn't get away with that for long, and soon I was reassigned to "the mean big sister." I tried to convince Katie that the mean big sister should go to her room for a nap, but she didn't go for it.

"No, let's say you push all those buttons," she said, indicating the radio dials, "and I see you and give you a time-out." That would work. A person could catch some shut-eye during a time-out.

Trapped as we were in the car by the pouring rain, time seemed to stand still, but just as Katie began to tire of drawing Pac-Man on the fogged-up windows, Amy's meeting let out.

Arriving home, I remembered the load of laundry in the dryer and rushed to get it out before all of Jerry's shirts became wrinkled to the point of needing ironing. And dinner would have to be something simple because now I wouldn't have time to prepare the chicken casserole I had planned on.

Jerry didn't get home until just before dinner, and when he sat down to his omelet, eyeing it a little critically, he reminded me that he had Back to School Night up at the junior high where he taught.

"Oh, that's right. What time do you have to leave?" I asked, thinking about the hopelessly wrinkled shirts in the laundry room and crossing my fingers that he wouldn't need one of them.

"In about ten minutes," he answered and ate his omelet without comment. A few minutes later, as Jerry was dressing to go out, I heard him call, "Hey, Julie! Where's my white shirt?"

Damn. "In the laundry room," I answered. "It just needs

to be ironed. I'll do it right now. It'll only take a minute." Frantically banging the iron around on his shirt, I said defensively, "I know you're wondering what I've been doing all day."

"No, I'm not," he answered, waiting patiently for me to finish with his shirt.

"Well, if I were home in the afternoons, I'd be more organized," I said, still feeling that I had to justify the omelet.

"Why aren't you home in the afternoons?"

"Oh, all Amy's extracurricular activities suddenly require additional meetings and rehearsals and practices. . . . " I trailed off, knowing what was coming.

"Well, you've got no one to blame for that but yourself."

"I know," I said resignedly. "But it's too late to do anything about it now."

"Oh, I can't believe that. There must be something you can cut out," he said, pulling on his shirt still warm from the iron. "Well, look, I've got to go. Thanks for the shirt." He adjusted his tie, ran a quick kiss across my cheek, called goodbye to the girls, and was gone. And while I stood there pondering what could be cut from Amy's routine, I knew that Jerry probably wouldn't even remember this conversation. Such is life.

Wednesday was no less hectic. Although ordinarily it was a "free" day, there was a soccer practice. We picked up hamburgers from McDonald's on the way home.

"Where have you guys been?" Jerry asked somewhat accusingly as we came in carrying bags reeking of french fries and onions.

"Soccer practice," I said simply.

"Oh," he said, and again ate his dinner without comment.

Thursday was Kitchen Chemistry and Friday the extra Brownie meeting before Saturday's Octoberfest. By the end of the week Katie and I had spent more time in the car than out of it. I had filled the gas tank twice, and Jerry hardly touched his corn dogs at Friday night's dinner.

Saturday dawned bright and sunny. At breakfast Jerry asked, "So do we have plans for today or what?" Amy and I exchanged glances. Hopeless.

"Today is the Octoberfest downtown. Amy's Brownie troop has a booth and is doing an authentic German folk dance at noon," I explained.

"Oh. I didn't know that was today."

"And at three o'clock is her championship soccer game," I added.

"Today?" Jerry asked incredulously.

"You got it."

"That seems a bit much. I thought you were going to cut back on some of this stuff, Julie."

"I'm working on it. But there are a lot of things to be considered."

I was relieved when he let it go at that. I would do some "considering" this weekend and see if there wasn't some solution to the situation.

What the Books Said

We didn't have to be at the Octoberfest until eleven o'clock, so while the kids were watching their usual Saturday-morning Smurfathon, I sat down with a few good books, the first of which was *Ask Dr. Salk.* Momentarily at a loss as to what index entry to look under, I decided to try "Extracurricular activities." Nope, "Exaggeration" was as close as I could get. But the Table of Contents listed the topic of each question discussed, so I read through all 171 topics, which ranged from "Explaining Heart Attacks" to

"Helping an Infant in Pain," only to discover no significant lead. *Your Six Year Old* by Ames and Ilg spent so much time discussing how, or even whether, your child fit into first grade that I'm sure if the subject of extracurricular activities had come up, they would have nipped it in the bud. And while I learned all about enrichment through books (I made a note to read Thurber's *The Wonderful O),* music, and theater in *The Mother's Almanac,* I didn't find what I was looking for. Because the index of *Kids: Day In and Day Out* hopped from "Exploring Space with a Camera" to "Eyelet Refills, for crafts," I flipped back to the Contents listings. "Schools and Learning" would have to do. Needless to say this section was filled with arguments, suggestions, and personal recommendations on schools: private, public, co-operative, and alternative. I finally learned what exactly the Montessori Method was and I enjoyed Ms. Scharlatt's article "Why I'm Not Changing My Kid's School This Year Even Though I Hate a Lot of Things About It." But at no time did extracurricular activities enter into the articles I read.

About to give up, I decided to take one final stab and look in Joan Beck's *Effective Parenting.* Bingo, there it was, "Extra-curricular activities, pressure of." I flipped to page 315 and read, "In the beginning, it didn't seem like pressure, but opportunity. . . . Sally next door urged Debbie into signing up for those swimming lessons on Saturdays in the high-school pool. . . . Suddenly ten-year-old Debbie is scheduled from breakfast to bedtime. So is Debbie's mother, who is either chauffeuring or telephoning about the day's car-pool complexities, or reminding Debbie to practice or to remember her leotard or to feed the parakeets or just hurry-you'll-be-late. And life is filled not so much with opportunity as it is with pressure. There is no time to invite Barbara over just to play." Wow, it was the story of my life. And it wasn't so much Ms. Beck's advice that impressed me

(" . . . the trap of too many wonderful, worthwhile, enriching activities can snap shut on most of the after-school freedom, leaving them caught in a rat race. . . . ") as it was that these were ten- and eleven-year-olds she was referring to. Amy was not yet six and a half. That suddenly sounded very young by comparison, and I had the sinking feeling I'd fallen into another parental pitfall.

What Maggie Said

Just before the last Smurf episode Maggie called to let me know she was having a plant "open house." Her home plant parties had been a little slow getting off the ground, and her supervisor told her this was a good way to attract customers.

"I can't make it today, Maggie," I apologized. "Amy's got a Brownie thing at eleven and then a big soccer game at three. Sorry."

"I didn't know Amy was in soccer this year. I thought she was going to gymnastics."

"She is," I admitted.

"Oh." There was a pause before Maggie said, "Soccer, gymnastics, *and* Brownies? Gosh, Julie, I hope you're not overdoing it."

"Do you think it's too much?" I asked, a little embarrassed. Even though I felt dishonest not mentioning it, there was no way I would admit to Kitchen Chemistry now!

"Well, the truth of the matter is that *I'm* just not willing to put up with the inconvenience of shagging a kid here and there five days a week. I guess I'm just too selfish," Maggie concluded.

"Oh, come on, you can hardly call yourself selfish!" I objected.

"Oh, I know, but I have to be selfish for Megan and Ryan then, since they can't really stick up for themselves. Megan's preschool messes up Ryan's schedule enough as it is. If I had to dash out every afternoon with Amanda, he'd never have a decent nap."

"Yeah, I know what you mean. You wouldn't believe the hours Katie and I have spent in the car this past week."

"See? And is that fair to her? Regardless of whether you're overburdening Amy, don't overburden yourself!"

"But I thought Amanda *was* in Brownies this year. We discussed it."

"She is. But her meetings are just down the street and she walks. *And* she's doing ballet, but it's ages five to seven, so I snuck Megan in the class even though she won't be five for another four months," Maggie explained. And when she continued it was almost as if she were talking to herself. "I'm tempted to give Amanda piano lessons, though, because we could have someone come to the house. But I should probably hold off for another year. . . . I wonder though, what about Spanish?" And then, turning her attention back to me, she said, "It's hard not to overdo, isn't it? If I didn't have Ryan holding me back, I'd probably be in your shoes right now. But you've got to consider yourself and the rest of your family. The Amys and Amandas of the world need to learn that other people have rights too. Even if it's just the right to sleep!"

"Good point, Maggie," I said. Yes, that appealed to the humanistic side of me.

"Well, listen, I'll let you go. I know you're *busy,* and I've got a bunch more phone calls to make."

"Good luck on your plant sale, and thanks a lot for the advice."

"Any time! Bye-bye."

Hmmm. So now it had become a human rights issue.

What My Mother Said

Being the good grandparents they are, my mother and father joined us at the Octoberfest, applauded vigorously, and took lots of pictures. Heading back to our car at about half past one, my mother asked me what we were doing that afternoon and if we'd like to come to dinner.

"Amy's got her big championship soccer game this afternoon. But we should be home by four-thirty or five. Dinner sounds fine."

"On, no, that's silly. You'll all be too tired. Look at poor Katie. She's dragging now. Will she have time for a nap?" My mother was big on naps.

"She can rest for a while when we get home," I said.

My mother shook her head and said, "It's not the same as a *nap*."

"I don't know what the big concern is over Katie. Amy's the one who has to play the game," I answered defensively.

"I know, but Amy thrives on pressure. She'll push herself to the limit for you and never say a word. But when she starts developing nervous tics and can't get to sleep at night because she's afraid she'll run out of air, then you'll have no one to blame but yourself." Now, where had I heard that phrase before?

This was tough talk, coming from my mother. Her usual supportive comments were conspicuously absent from the conversation.

"I take it you think I've overdone on Amy's extracurricular activities," I said.

"Well, since you brought it up, yes, I do. Julie, honey, she's not even six and a half. She's got her whole life to play soccer."

"I know, you're right," I conceded. "But she seems to

enjoy it, and how was I to know her team'd be league champions?"

"She enjoys it because you and Jerry want her to. She'd do anything to please you, but believe me, a six-year-old kid ought to come home from school and play. And that's all."

"No Brownies?"

"Is it really necessary?"

"You're asking me?"

She laughed and slipped her arm around my waist. "You know how I am," she said. "I just hate to see the girls grow up too fast."

"You always say that. Amy'll be eighteen years old and you'll be wringing your hands because she's too young to be wearing a two-piece bathing suit."

"Oh! I don't even want to think about it!" she cried, and we both laughed.

"But seriously, Julie," my mother cautioned, "look at the dark circles under Amy's eyes. You've got to help her. You're her mother and that's what mothers do."

"I suppose it is," I answered. Yes, I *had* noticed Amy's dark circles at dinner the other night, and I knew from past experience that it was a telltale sign of nervous tension. "It's a good thing you're around to keep me in line, Mom," I said, smiling.

"Oh, you're a wonderful mom, you know that. Look at those darling girls." For a few moments we both watched Amy and Katie walking hand in hand with Grandpa and Jerry. Amy was singing her Octoberfest song while Katie trudged steadily along beside her. Jerry and my father were having a deep discussion on foreign affairs. As if she knew we were watching her, Katie turned and caught my eye.

"Momma, my legs are tired," she said. Jerry stopped in

midsentence and offered, "Do you want to ride on my shoulders?"

High above the crowd of festival-goers Katie swung her legs contentedly and flashed us a happy smile.

"Yeah, they are cute, aren't they?" I commented proudly. We reached our cars, and as we prepared to go our separate ways, my mother called to Amy, "Good luck on your soccer game, honey!" and to me she said, "Let me know about dinner. Don't worry, we'll keep it simple!"

"Okay, I'll call you. And thanks, Mom, for everything."

What My Husband Said

Jerry was watching the last half of *Sixty Minutes* when I came downstairs, having tucked the kids into bed.

"They were *tired*," I said, sinking down onto the couch beside him.

"Busy weekend," he answered.

"Too busy, do you think?"

"I think you've got Amy doing too much, if that's what you mean."

It was.

"So what should she drop? Everything? C'mon and give me a hand here. She's your daughter too."

He turned his attention away from Dan Rather, who was raking some poor health-spa owner over the coals, and answered, "Okay, I'd like to see her continue the gymnastics. She's getting quite good, and it will give her something to feel special about. I think soccer should wait until she's at least ten or eleven, and I don't have an opinion one way or another about Brownies. But if it involves a lot of days like yesterday, forget it."

"No, Octoberfest comes but once a year," I said, trying to shed some humor on his speech. "Soccer's over now anyway. I'll ask Amy if she wants to drop Kitchen Chemistry. That would settle things down."

"Sounds good," said Jerry, and I could tell he had dismissed the problem.

Andy Rooney was on now, and we sat comfortably side by side watching him go through the contents of his car glove compartment.

"He cracks me up," I said as he pulled out a pair of sunglasses with only one lense.

"I wonder what he makes doing this show?" Jerry always wondered what people made at such seemingly trivial, however entertaining, occupations.

"More than you make, that's for sure," I answered.

He laughed and said, "*Everyone* makes more than I do, Julie."

"That's true," I agreed, getting up to fix us some dessert.

What I Did

Amy opted to pass on the remaining four weeks of Kitchen Chemistry. Turns out it was "kind of boring because all the boys stood on the desks and wouldn't pay attention to the teacher." And for this Katie and I played house in the car?

And when Donna called about Amy's obvious enrollment in the upcoming soccer clinic, I held my ground. I told her we were moving.

We stayed with Brownies and gymnastics but bowed out of the anniversary celebration and its numerous rehearsals. Life slowed to a comfortable pace. Katie could rest quietly in the afternoons, Amy had time to play in the rain-filled gutters with her friends, and Jerry was getting decent dinners again.

One afternoon a blue slip of paper came home with Amy's spelling dictation. It was a reminder that the Aquatics Club Swim Team sign-ups would be held this coming Saturday. The flier said all the right things, pushed all the right buttons. The center of the page was devoted to a dramatic picture of a beautifully poised swimmer. The caption read, "Swimming: The Sport of Champions." My heart picked up an extra beat and my hands became predictably sticky.

"I must be crazy," I said to myself. Disgusted, I tossed the announcement into the trash. All afternoon long and into the evening, each time I reached under the sink to throw something away, I caught a glimpse of that swimmer frozen in perfect position with one arm curved gracefully above his head. Definitely champion material.

It wasn't until I threw out the empty ice-cream carton that I finally succeeded in covering him up. And even then, one small green corner containing the words "sign up" remained to taunt me. It was a test. I knew that. But I had passed.

7

Deciding on Discipline

It's hard to say exactly when the struggle for power begins. Are those cries that bring you to the cribside in the first few months solely cries of hunger, discomfort, and excess energy, or does the power play really begin at birth? I imagine this theory has been researched, documented, and thoroughly analyzed by the experts, but since a baby can't talk and then, when finally able to talk, can't remember those early months, it's all academic, isn't it?

However, you *can* be sure that the toy tossed out of the crib, the spoon thrown down from the highchair, and the bottle innocently dropped from the stroller are definite attempts to draw you, the parent, into the inevitable contest for control.

It was at this stage of babyhood that I recognized the need to set standards, establish a consistent approach to discipline that would lay the groundwork for the bigger battles ahead. I mean, if you can't control an eight-month-old, what'll you do when she's thirteen years old? So, with my usual air of superiority I went about setting limits and determining reasonable expectations. But it wasn't long before I discovered that it was a lot harder to train Amy not to eat the houseplants than I'd thought. And there were other issues, too, like waking in the night, refusing to sit in the car seat, and resisting naps that became challenges beyond my wildest imagination. We were more successful at some than at others, Jerry and I, and weathered those early storms lying side by side in bed at night reassuring each other we were doing the right thing. In the dark I would strain to hear the confidence in Jerry's voice that I always counted on to get us through. Fooled at first into thinking that we would always "win" because we were bigger, stronger, and smarter, we failed to take into account her endless stream of energy that would wear us down and her mind like a steel trap that never forgot the slightest mistake. That was how she often beat us at our own game.

Yet there's more than one way to skin a cat, as the saying goes, and in the years to follow we experimented with a variety of disciplinary techniques.

In the beginning there were charts. Yes, charts, with their rows of brightly colored stars reinforcing such good behavior as Brushed Teeth, Picked Up Toys, and Ate Vegetables, came highly recommended and promised to modify even the worst of habits. The trick was to list several things that the child already did well and then slip in the one or two things that you wanted to encourage. In our first experience with charts we wanted three-year-old Amy to stop squeezing, pinching, bumping, and generally annoying six-month-old Katie. So, mixed into such sure things as Looked at Books, Washed Hair, and Played Outside was Be Gentle to Katie. Since Amy was too young to read these entries, we had cut out magazine pictures resembling the activities and glued them to the chart. As the days passed a definite pattern appeared. Stars for Playing Outside, Washed Hair, and Looked at Books stretched clear across the sheet. But there was one gaping hole that stood out from clear across the room. Closer inspection revealed the area of difficulty to be—you guessed it—Be Gentle to Katie. At first, stars were intermittently scattered in the row adjacent to the cartoon baby with one small hair curling from the top of its head; then all is lost and there's nothing but blank paper. That's how it is with charts. Instead of being a tribute to a child's successes, they soon become an embarrassment, with blank spaces that expose a child's weak points and remind her of her failures.

And then there's the problems of rewards. While the younger child may not figure it out, the five-year-old is bound to ask, "What do I get for all these stars?" This question requires careful consideration. Big rewards take lots of stars and therefore often self-destruct before the goal has been reached. Either that or it takes so long to earn it that the child loses interest in the whole system. And yet, while short-term rewards almost guarantee some kind of success, the parent is still stuck with finding some small yet treasured item that will ruin neither the child's teeth or the family's budget. Am I right? But it's worth a try. And before the novelty wore off, I think we really did make some progress. At least you can be sure Amy had the cleanest hair in the neighborhood! And she also received our attention in a positive way, which is probably all she wanted in the first place.

As the chart began to lose its effectiveness, however, we decided to try a new approach. We entered into the age of isolation. Ah, yes, the old-fashioned command "Go to your room!" now translated into "Take a time-out!" It was heaven. It felt good to be taking some kind of affirmative action against undesirable behavior. Enough of this goody-two-shoes here's-a-star-for-breathing stuff. I took to time-outs like a duck to water.

By this time Amy was in preschool and Katie just entering her second year. Preschools are big on time-outs, so it was easy to follow it up at home. Of course Amy would have died a thousand deaths were she given a time-out at school, but at home, well, that was another story . . . you know how it is. So, for grabbing a toy from Katie, for refusing to share with a friend, or for arguing about who got to drink from the Flintstone cup, Amy received the usual sentence of ten minutes. For a time-out to be effective, though, it can't be 'fun. For that reason we soon dropped the policy of sending Amy to her room for the required period. It never failed that when we'd call her ten minutes later to rejoin us, she'd answer no thanks; she was busy playing. Another key ingredient to the time-out is the timer. Not only does grabbing up the timer, giving it a sharp twist to the ten-minute mark, and slamming it down on the kitchen table give you something to do with hands that are itching to swat the kid, but it also prevents you from forgetting her until she calls a half an hour later from the dining room, "Can I get up now?" And if you place the timer so that she can see it (but not touch it, or those minutes may just fly by, if you know what I mean), she won't have to ask "How much longer do I have to sit here?" every thirty seconds, which is probably more irritating than what it was she did to get there in the first place!

All in all, we found time-outs to diffuse potentially angry scenes as well as to impress upon Amy that unacceptable behavior meant exclusion from family and friends. There are, however, a few time-out pitfalls. The first and most obvious is, of course, overkill. If the time-outs are too long or too frequent, they lose effect and become an issue in themselves. I think Dennis the Menace has proved that point. Another thing you want to avoid is the captive-audience lecture. Plunked down in time-out, Amy was easy prey for a "talking to," and I found these opportunities hard to resist. It probably wouldn't have been so bad if I'd stuck to the issue at hand, but I usually wound up dragging whether or not she had made her bed that morning into the conversation. Therefore, before I got around to feeding the cat before dinner, she had long since tuned me out and I was angrier than when she had first sat down. So, for this system to work, you either need a lot of self-control or a special time-out site out of earshot. And when it came Katie's turn to suffer the humiliation of a time-out, she would hop up onto the chair only too happy to take a break from the hustle and bustle of play. You can fool some of the people some of the time. . . .

But isolating Amy when she demonstrated negative behavior did not, nor did we expect it to, change that behavior. For that we would eventually apply behavior modification. It was actually B. F. Skinner who got the ball rolling on this theory when he trained rats to press levers to get food, back in the 1930s. Only he called it instrumental conditioning. Whatever. It all amounts to the same thing, getting kids (rats . . . what's the difference?) to do something because of what happens after they do it. But what makes behavior modification difficult is the challenge of catching kids in the act of being good. It isn't a be-nice-to-your-sister-for-a-day/ hour/minute-and-I'll-buy-you-an-ice-cream kind of deal (i.e., bribe), but rather a scientifically proven approach to tricking children into being good.

So when we finally faced the fact that Amy was entirely too bossy (at age six she wore her "Born to Boss" T-shirt with real pride), we decided to give it a whirl. I supplied myself with several packages of stickers; some Snoopy, some Star Wars, and one batch of Scratch 'n Sniff, and began lurking around corners, hiding behind houseplants, and sneaking down hallways in an attempt to catch Amy being, shall we say, cooperative. Not an easy assignment, but when I finally did hear her husky voice acknowledge that someone other than herself actually had a good idea, I appeared instantly on the scene and handed her a sticker of Snoopy holding a bunch of balloons that spelled out "You're A Winner!" She was thrilled. Ah, thank goodness for the craze that has made something as simple as a sticker the reward of the eighties.

"What's this for?" she asked.

"For being so cooperative with your friends," I said smugly and slipped quietly from the room. You could have heard a pin drop.

I continued my vigilance in the weeks to follow, my back pressed against the wall as I strained to hear the Candyland game in progress, making trip after trip through the playroom, pretending to put the laundry away, waiting and watching for Amy to push that lever and get her reward. And my efforts were not in vain. She got the hint and began cooperating more and more in hopes of my being within earshot of her good deeds. In fact, so successful was the program that I decided to apply it to another area of concern. Amy had developed the annoying habit of having an answer for everything. If you said, "Put your bike in the garage," she would say, "I only rode it once. Missy left it out there." Or, if she were to ask, "Mom, can I go over to Jimmy's to see his new hamster?" and I were to answer "No, it's too close to dinner," there'd be the standard, "But Mom, you said . . ." Not a catastrophic problem, I'll admit, but it's often these little irritants that become the final straw. And the nice part about this assignment was that it required less sneaking around. A simple "Okay, Mom" would earn Amy the coveted fuzzy bear sticker. Unfortunately, once she figured out the right lever to push, she came up with a plan to rig the experiment. She'd ask to do something that she knew I'd say no to and then, when I did, she'd brightly respond, "Okay, Mom!" and wait expectantly for her pellet . . . er, sticker. Oh, well, some rats are quicker than others.

So I turned my attention to Katie. She being the baby of the family, and generally more laid back than Amy, we had allowed her to slide on a few of the finer points. Whereas Amy had been expected to say "please" and "thank you" from the time she could talk, Katie was still getting away with "I need something to drink," and she got it too. So, the levers being determined, we set about to modify her behavior. It wasn't long before "please" and "thank you" were incorporated into Katie's daily speech pattern, and I was feeling quite impressed with B. F. Skinner until Katie asked at dinner, "Are we still playing that sticker game?" It occurred to me then that the change in our expectations probably had more to do with her newfound manners than did the stack of stickers on her bedside table.

But like most things in life, when it gets easier, you don't try as hard. And so it was with us. Because things were going so smoothly, we relaxed our vigil, let down our guard, and generally took it easy for a while. Big mistake. There is no such thing as taking it easy when it comes to discipline. And several months later we found ourselves back to square one, only this time the problem was the classic "I have to tell them to go brush their teeth a hundred times before they finally do it." Oh, I know what you're thinking: If I didn't *tell* them a hundred times, it wouldn't *take* them that many. Right? Other people's mistakes are so obvious, aren't they? But they're never that simple when they're your own.

I learned this lesson one afternoon as I was making preparations for a family evening at a friend's house. Admittedly, kids are easier to organize the older they get, but they still need to be bathed and probably fed since they won't like what's for dinner anyhow. Pajamas and "lovies" need to be packed just in case we decide to stay late, and that includes toothbrushes and toothpaste. And then you have to get yourself ready and finish making the salad or dessert that you said you'd bring but now wish you hadn't. And no matter when you begin these preparations, you will inevitably run late.

On this particular day I was doing fine until the rabbit escaped from its cage and hid behind the big poky yucca plant in the backyard. Recapturing him set me back ten minutes, and I lost another fifteen when my neighbor came over to borrow some children's aspirin and told me she was leaving her husband. This opened up eight years' worth of frustration. I think I got off easy with fifteen minutes. So when I went in search of Amy and Katie, I was in no mood for games.

Coming into the family room, I was surprised to see the floor littered with books. "These books need to be picked up before we go out tonight," I said to Amy and Katie, who were busy coloring. And then, because I was—you got it—running late, I left to take my shower before making sure that my directions were carried out. When I returned fifteen minutes later the books were still all over the floor.

"I thought I told you to pick up these books," I said accusingly.

"Oh, I didn't know you meant *now*." Amy answered coolly. Her eyes never left the page she was carefully outlining.

"Well, I did. Pick them up and then I'll start your bath. We're late as it is!" As I stomped off to finish dressing I warned, "I'll be back in five minutes!"

Ten minutes later (everything a mother does takes twice as long as she thinks it will) I reappeared at the doorway, only to find the books still strewn across the room. Other than switching from green to blue, Amy hadn't budged. It was possible that Katie had made an attempt to pick up but then became bogged down when she came across a favorite book.

"What is going on here?" I demanded. "You guys make me so mad! I ask you to do one simple thing, pick up books. Is that too much to ask?" And while I ranted I gathered up books, shoving them furiously onto shelves and into drawers. Amy and Katie watched me blitz the room from a safe distance, and feeling their gaze upon me, I turned and shouted, "So get over here and help pick up this room! Now!" They both jumped up and began gathering books and trying to look busy even though in my anger I had already done most of it myself.

Both children were fairly subdued after this outburst, bathing themselves silently and even allowing me to comb out their hair with the pink comb they hated because it "scraped their heads." Of course I chose the pink comb on purpose, deliberately tugging at their tangles in a passive-aggressive attempt to punish them. Now, how sick can you get?

Thoroughly disgusted with myself and my kids, I piled everyone into the car and drove off. But soon, soothed by the warmth of the afternoon sun as it came through the glass window beside me, I began to relax and contemplate the affirmative action I would take in the future to avoid such scenes. Let's see, I could set up a chart for each girl and list "Did As I Was Told The First Time I Was Told" as an entry, but somehow the idea didn't thrill me. And a time-out would only let them off the hook. Behavior modification might work. And I made a mental note to pick up some stickers in case I began such a campaign. Not to be ruled out, though, was the spanking. Ah, but a quick smack on the seat of their pants would feel good about now. To me, at least. Well, it beats yanking at snarls with a pink comb. Then there were more philosophical approaches to consider, like the family circle, the compromise, or natural consequences. Hey, I've read all the books. And perhaps part of the problem is that there are so many methods and theories that it's impossible to know what's best. But I decided that first thing in the morning I'd take another look anyway.

What the Books Said

You can tell a lot about a book by its terminology. Spock refers to discipline as "Managing Young Children," while the index of Dreikus's *The Challenge of Parenthood* has a cross-reference to "Training." And Joan Beck doesn't list "Discipline" at all, but prefers the phrase "Disobedience, handling of"—bless her heart. Whatever they call it, they all love to talk about it, listing page numbers for everything from "in the car" to "washing the mouth." The thought of sorting through all this information was overwhelming. *The Mother's Almanac* had seventy-four entries alone, and even Spock, accused of being liberal more because of his antiwar philosophy than his ideas on discipline, had twenty-five. But I was still mad at him for telling me Katie's life wasn't satisfying enough, so I didn't bother looking up "Excessive need to punish" or "Parental guilt." Who needs it?

I stood in front of the bookshelf staring at the same old titles. Dobson's *The Strong-Willed Child* was tempting, but I'd already *read* it (a lot of good it did me, too). Then there was a long stretch of parenting books devoted entirely to discipline. They ranged from such namby-pamby titles as

How to Discipline with Love and *Between Parent and Child*
to the more assertive *Dare to Discipline* and *How to Get
Your Children to Do What You Want Them to Do*. Actually,
the last was one of Jerry's books that he used in his drug-
abuse prevention workshops for parents. I pulled it down
from the shelf and placed it on his desk alongside *Parents,
Peers and Pot, Tough Love,* and *Back in Control.* Whew!
There was some heavy reading. But tired of sifting through
the opinions of the more conventional authors, I decided to
read Paul Wood's *How to Get Your Children to Do What
You Want Them to Do* book. I spent the next hour and a
half reading and learned more and felt more confident than
I had in a long time. I knew right from the start that I'd come
to the right place when Dr. Wood, in explaining why his
book was relatively short (barely 100 pages) stated,
"Though much of what has [already] been written is valuable, a few key points in understanding and correcting
behavioral problems have been totally missed. It seems to
be a case of not being able to see the forest for the trees. In
the course of analyzing parental difficulties, we have too
often lost the total picture. This we have found to be true of
psychoanalytically-oriented books which often help parents
understand their child, but still not know how to deal with
him; and with behavior modification type books which
frequently leave parents frustrated in their efforts to find a
suitable reward or punishment with which to change their
child's behavior." He then proceeds to spell out a step-by-
step approach to getting your children to do what you want
them to do. "Say what you mean—Meaning what you say"
is an important part of the program as well as establishing
clear goals. As I read through the various case histories, it
became obvious to me that my own goal—"These books
need to be picked up"—was not a goal at all, but a
statement. By the time I got to chapter 4, "Where to Start

with Your Child," I was convinced I could change problem behavior. I copied the Intervention Worksheet from the back of the book and began filling in Step 1: Listing Problem Behaviors. Yep, I'd have these kids shaped up in no time.

Just out of curiosity, though, I thumbed through Greg Bodenhamer's *Back in Control*. And again clear directions were imperative. Effective follow-through, though, was also another important element in getting kids to behave. As Mr. Bodenhamer points out, "If punishment succeeded at changing behavior, we wouldn't have to keep using it." He concludes the chapter by stating, "Don't punish. Instead, effectively follow through." The other big parental pitfall *Back in Control* warns parents against is inconsistency. Mr. Bodenhamer asks, "Are your children likely to be consistent in obeying rules that you aren't consistent in enforcing?" There were charts at the back of the book too. The Daily Plan included the week's mandatory behavior, the clearly stated rule, the planned follow-through, and the planned consistency.

Closing *Back in Control* I glanced at the two remaining books on Jerry's desk. *Tough Love* had a picture of a fist wrapped around a heart. . . . I didn't think that at ages four and six it had come to that. That left *Parents, Peers and Pot.* One thing at a time, I told myself, one thing at a time.

What Maggie Said

Maggie, having given up on her home plant parties, called to fill me in on her newest venture, Mary Kay Cosmetics.

"I'm giving a demonstration Thursday night. Hope you can make it."

My heart sank. The last thing in the world I needed was blusher or lip liner. But you know how it is, I felt an obligation as a friend. And I never knew when I'd be giving a Tupperware party.

"Thursday? Sure, that sounds fine," I faked enthusiasm.

"That is, if I can get this place cleaned up by then. I must have told the kids fifty times today to pick up the upstairs. It's a losing battle." Maggie sighed.

"You too, huh? We had that fight last night. What do you think the answer is?"

"Oh, Julie, don't ask me. We just go from threats to bribes and back to threats again." And then she added quietly, "And they're both so destructive."

"What do you mean?" I asked, feeling I'd touched a real sore spot.

"Well, you're just asking for trouble with a threat. It's a challenge few kids can resist testing, and then when they do, you're stuck with either following through on some ludicrous statement like 'If you tease your sister again you'll be in your room for a week,' or you've got to back down. A declaration of defeat they never let you forget."

"Yeah, you really have to think a threat through. Not an easy thing to do when you're mad, either," I agreed. "But what about bribes? I thought Tom was into bribes." I laughed. We had this joke between us. Tom loved his bribes as much as Jerry did his consequences.

"He *is*. That's the problem, Julie. He's got the kids so conditioned that they won't do a *thing* unless there's something in it for them. It's disgusting." There was that sore spot again. "So he bribes them and I threaten them. What can I say?" Maggie added with a dry laugh. Poor Maggie. It's hard enough to discipline kids without having conflicting techniques muddying the waters.

"Listen, I just read a really terrific book. It's called, and you'll love this, *How to Get Your Children to Do What You Want Them to Do.*"

"Never heard of it."

"It's one of Jerry's books for school that I just happened to come across. It's a real eye-opener, Maggie, and the best part is you can read it in a morning."

"Well, pass it along. I could use some new material."

"I'll bring it with me on Thursday. And have Tom read it too. It really will help." Maggie was always so helpful whenever I called to pick her brain that I was glad I could reciprocate this once and send some good advice her way. "In fact," I added, "I'll loan you *two* books. Jerry has a copy of *Back in Control* that has some excellent ideas in it."

"Great! I feel better already just knowing help is on the way."

"Yeah, now you know how the pioneers must have felt when they heard the bugle call of the cavalry coming to save them from an Indian attack," I said, laughing.

"Really, that's not too far from the truth in this house!"

"Well, don't scalp anyone before Thursday, Maggie," I answered, and we said our goodbyes in considerably better moods than we had our hellos.

What My Mother Said

Remembering that my mother sometimes used Mary Kay Cosmetics, I called her to see if there was anything I could get for her Thursday. That would solve my problem of ordering something I didn't necessarily want.

"Oh, what perfect timing," my mother said when I mentioned Maggie's demonstration. "I'm down to my last drop of the moisture cream. You can get me some more, and I'll stop by on Friday after I get my hair done to pick it up." And then she added, "Oh, goody! An excuse to come by and squeeze Katie!"

"God, you're so sicko," I said, but I was forever thankful that she felt that way. "Anyway," I said in a proud voice, "I'll have them so shaped up by then you won't recognize them."

"Oh, no, *now* what are you putting those girls through? Not another chart, please tell me it's not a chart!" she pleaded dramatically.

"No, it's not another chart," I said, mimicking her tone. "In fact it's nothing like that really," I continued. "I've just read a couple of books that gave me some new insights into getting kids to do what you want them do do."

"You know, your father and I didn't have all these books when we were raising you kids. At least I never read any of them. Spock, I guess, was the only one I'd ever heard of. And in some ways I think it was easier that way."

"I know what you mean. It is hard to sort through all the different theories, especially the way the psychologists keep changing their minds, but I think I've got a live one this time." I laughed.

"Well, you do what you think is best, but I don't even see where there's a problem."

"That's because you're a grandmother. But you have to admit that Amy has her moments."

"True. But nothing a good swat on the bottom wouldn't solve. You know how I feel, Julie. There's too much talking where Amy's concerned."

"That's why you'll like this new system. It cuts down on unnecessary discussion. In fact, Greg Bodenhamer recommends you say nothing more than the clear direction itself," I explained.

"I like the sound of that, but you might want to consider a spanking to go along with it," she persisted, and then added, "But now that I think about it, you never did get a spanking, just your brothers."

"Oh, I remember being spanked. Not that it ever did any good," I teased. "I also remember being chased up the stairs with the broom!"

"I never did that! You're making that up!" she insisted. We continued reminiscing a few minutes longer and then hung up with promises to see each other Friday.

What My Husband Said

Equipped with both a Daily Plan and a Family Intervention Worksheet, I approached Jerry Tuesday evening about filling them out with me.

"The Daily Plan is from *Back in Control,*" I explained. "And this one is from *How to Get Your Children to Do What You Want Them to Do,*" I said, indicating the Intervention Worksheet.

"You mean you *finally* read them?" Jerry asked, surprised.

"What do you mean?"

"Those are the two books I suggested you read a long time ago. Remember? I got them for that parenting class. I *told* you they were good."

"*Those* were the books you wanted me to read?" Now it was my turn to be surprised. "I thought you were trying to push some boring psychological study off on me."

Ignoring my last remark, Jerry said, "Now you know why I've been chanting, 'Say what you mean, mean what you say,' all month."

It was true. Every time I had some sort of run-in with the kids he'd say that to me. And, to be honest, it was getting damn irritating! But now that I understood where it came from, I could see his point.

"So let's fill these out," I said, getting back on the subject. I wanted to avoid a review of my disciplinary techniques for the past month.

"Well, I don't think we need both. Let's use Bodenhamer's because it has a 'follow-through' section." He took the sheet from my hands and placed it on the table in front of us. "This week's mandatory behavior," he read out loud. "What do you think?" he asked. "Follow directions?"

"That's too vague," I answered. "How about 'Pick up room when told,'" I suggested, thinking about our most recent fracas.

But picking up the pencil, Jerry wrote, "Do what you are told the first time you are told to do it."

"Oh, Jerry," I criticized, "that's too much to expect."

"That's the problem with you, Julie. Your expectations aren't high enough. You don't give these kids enough credit."

"I just think you've got to have reasonable expectations. Otherwise they're trying to do the impossible, and that's self-defeating," I said, holding my own.

"Julie, you need to get a clearer picture of what these kids are capable of. There's no reason on earth why they can't do as they're told the first time they're told. And if we present a united front and let them know what's expected, it'll work."

"Okay." I'm sure Jerry was right. He usually is. Perhaps I should reread Paul Wood's chapter "Viewing Your Child As Capable of Changing His Behavior."

We finished filling in the chart and decided to discuss it with the girls the next afternoon. I liked having a plan of action. I liked working together. But I couldn't seem to shake the feeling that something was missing. I didn't know what exactly, but it would come to me.

What I Did

Now, let me see if I've got this straight. Determine the expected behavior, use clear directions to say what you mean, then consistently and effectively follow through on those clearly stated goals. Have I left anything out? Whew! I feel like a kid in school putting spelling words into a sentence. But we put our plan into action and worked hard on it. Amy and Katie actually flourished under the new management, and it made me realize how important structure is to a child. Things quieted down around here. It was nice, pleasant even. And that made Amy and Katie so much easier to love.

And then it came to me, what it was that was missing before. It was love. The real genuine kind that gushes from your heart at such a rate that it hurts. It was missing because love dries up to a trickle when all you feel is anger and frustration. And if you think about it, it works both ways. If it's hard to love a child who constantly whines or argues, then it's also hard for a child to love a parent who's always yelling or threatening. That realization motivated me to continue with our new course of action because regardless of what we all say about independence and freedom, without that bond of love there is only emptiness.

So it *is* worth the effort. Effort? We're talking struggle, strain, and strife. No part of parenthood is as difficult as the job of disciplinarian because no one can be *that* sure and *that* strong all the time. That's why mothers invented making up. It must have been a mother who first slipped into her child's darkened room to ask forgiveness. Only a mother would humble herself just to kiss that soft cheek and feel those small arms wrap tightly around her neck, telling it all. Yes, let the experts tell us how to do it right, but leave it to a mother to know what to do when it goes wrong.

So we persevered with clear goals and effective follow-through, but when human nature got the better of me and I succumbed to arguments, door-slamming, and, yes, the pink comb ("No, no, anything but the pink comb!"), I always found a way to make up. Children are really more forgiving than we realize, wanting those hugs and gentle words as much as we do.

8

The Problem
with Pets

"Think of it as 'Pet Therapy,'"
I said to Jerry during one of our many discussions, in which
I discuss and he doesn't, about whether or not we should
get a dog. A little puppy . . . for Katie, really. Because it was
Katie, now five, who had turned out to be the real animal
lover of the family. It made sense, really, considering her
checkered past of make-believe friends and teddy-bear
companions.

"I know I'm going to regret this, but 'Pet Therapy'?"

"Sure, children learn to express their feelings through the
pet. You know, Katie's preschool teacher told us she had a
hard time opening up to adults. . . . Well, this might help," I
concluded, rather proud of my theory.

"You don't really expect me to buy that, do you?" Jerry
laughed.

"I guess not," I admitted, a little disappointed. But was I
really so naive to have thought he'd go for it? This was a
man who referred to dogs as an "emergency food source."

He felt that dogs were out of place in suburban life, that they belonged out on ranches or farms, earning their keep. And in some ways I had to agree with him. There's nothing more irritating than a dog that's been penned up all day and then let out at dusk to run loose through the neighborhood, scaring small children—and worse, if you know what I mean. Or the dog that barks so long and loud during the night you'd swear it was just below the bedroom window.

"Well, I agree that the suburban dog may not earn his keep rounding up sheep or chasing off rabbits, but he has a special worth all his own," I argued, quite convincingly too, if I may say. "If well trained and treated kindly, he can become a valuable member of the family." I rested my case.

"Kind of like your aunt Winnie, who thinks she's a cat, huh?" You could tell he was pleased to have thought of that.

"Very funny, but you can wipe that smirk off your face because she doesn't have that problem any more."

"Oh, darn, I wanted to ask her what she did about fur balls!" He was on a roll now.

"Will you stop it!" I cried, trying not to laugh. "I'm not through talking about dogs!"

"Well, I am. Julie, the answer is no."

Following him into the kitchen, I ignored his last remark and said, "A dog offers companionship, loyalty . . ."

"Fleas, vet bills, carpet stains . . . Julie, you're not listening."

"I know, because you're not saying what I want to hear," I sulked.

"I know you think you can badger me into this, like you did with the cat, but I'm *not* budging and you might as well face it." I could see that he meant it and any further harassment would only make him mad, so I decided to drop the subject . . . for now. But, feeling the need to defend his position, Jerry continued, "It's not like they've never had any pets. We've been through how many rats? Four? Five? And what about those snakes that ate the live goldfish? And they've got Tuffy! What more do you want?"

"A dog—a furry little puppy with a hard, round belly and sharp white teeth that will nibble on fingers and thrash socks from side to side," I answered.

"That's right!" he said, delighted at my unfortunate reference to thrashed socks. "They're destructive, too!"

"Okay, okay, you win," I conceded.

"What I don't understand is why you want to go through all the heartache of having a dog. Look at the agonies we've suffered just over those rats, not to mention the time Tuffy disappeared."

"Oh, that was so awful. But do you remember her bee sting? When her paw swelled up to five times its natural size?"

"Gosh, I'd forgotten all about that," Jerry said in that faraway voice people use when thinking of something long since past.

Tuffy couldn't have been more than ten weeks old when, batting playfully at a bee against the sliding glass door, she was stung on the paw. I can be sure of the date, you see, because it was also the Sunday before the first day of school. Amy would be in the first grade. When we sat down to dinner, Amy noticed that Tuffy was licking and tugging at her paw, and by the time the dishes had been cleared from the table Tuffy's paw was the size of a Ping-Pong ball. She let out a feeble meow as we inspected her paw but made no attempt to move. Her eyes seemed bigger and glassier than normal. Not wanting to alarm the children, we told them Tuffy was fine and just needed to rest quietly until the swelling went down. But after sending Amy and Katie upstairs to play before their bath, I let my true colors show.

"Jerry! Look at this paw! What are we going to do?"

"What do you mean? We aren't going to 'do' anything. She'll be fine. Animals don't die from bee stings, for heaven's sake."

"How do you know? People do!" I insisted. "She's so little, maybe the poison *could* kill her. Look how lethargic she is. . . . Oh my God, I don't think she's breathing!"

We both rushed over to where Tuffy lay on the kitchen floor. Placing our hands along her back and side, we were relieved to feel the slow rise and fall of her lungs.

"Jesus Christ!" Jerry cried out as he took his first good look at her paw. It was now at least five times its normal size.

"Oh, Jerry! We have to do something!" I was beginning to panic.

"Julie, it's Sunday evening. No veterinarian will be in his office now. And I'm not going to spend fifty dollars on an emergency after-hours office visit," Jerry replied, having regained his composure.

"Oh, fine. Let the cat die the night before first grade. Don't worry that the death of the little kitten Amy loves so will spoil all the excitement of her first day, week, or even month of school," I answered sarcastically. Sometimes you could shame them into action.

"So what would you like me to do?" See?

"I want you to call a vet. I don't care what it costs. I don't want Amy to come downstairs in the morning, all dressed in her new school clothes, to find her cat stiff as a board," I answered.

Because he didn't want to see Amy and Katie hurt any more than I did, he went to look up the phone number of a local vet. I heard his deep voice rumbling in the bedroom and knew he was making the call. When he came out of the room I asked, "What did he say?"

"I got his answering service. They'll relay the message and have him call me back as soon as possible," he said.

"Oh." And then I added, "I'm glad you called."

"Yeah, well, we'll see," he answered gruffly.

It was only a matter of minutes before the vet returned Jerry's call. And again I could hear the low rumbling of his voice as he explained the situation. Amy and Katie had come back downstairs to check on Tuffy. Frightened by her deteriorating condition, they were on the verge of tears when Jerry emerged from the bedroom with good news.

"Well, the vet says that Tuffy will probably be just fine."

"Should we take her in?" I asked.

"He said it really isn't necessary. The poison from the sting is already in her bloodstream and she just has to weather it out."

"He couldn't give her a shot or anything?" I persisted.

"Apparently not."

"Oh."

We all four stood staring down at poor Tuffy with her dreadfully swollen paw turned up so as not to touch the floor.

"C'mon. Let her rest and she'll be fine in the morning. You heard what Daddy said."

And the next morning she was fine, and Amy went off to school in the big yellow bus without a hitch.

But the time Tuffy disappeared we didn't have it so easy. It was two weeks before Christmas, and when, after three days, the food in her bowl hadn't been touched (yuck), I began to worry. The kids, being busy with Christmas activities, hadn't really noticed. When Amy asked where Tuffy was, I would say that I just saw her go out. Jerry, however, thought they should be told. And as the days passed and Christmas drew closer, I had to agree with him. I mean, there hung Tuffy's stocking on the mantle. Was I supposed to stuff a dead cat's stocking? Would we really get away, on Christmas morning, with "I just saw her go out" when everyone knew how she loved wrapping paper, not to mention Christmas catnip? And waiting any longer would definitely put a damper on the holiday. *What* to tell them was another problem. Jerry was sure the coyotes had gotten her, while I clung to the hope that she had become trapped in someone's garage. But before I could break it to the children, I made Jerry search one more time through the bushes in the green belt behind our house. I just thought that her death might be easier to accept, and explain, if we had proof. But all he came up with were two old tennis balls and someone's left sneaker.

So we told them Tuffy was missing, and because I didn't want to give them any false hope, we told them she was probably—and this part really stuck in my throat—dead. Well, they wouldn't hear of it. It was an impossible truth, not to be taken lying down. They drew up signs describing Tuffy's most distinctive markings: one white paw (do you have any idea how many cats there must be with one white paw?), orange face, and long whiskers (that was Katie's contribution). "Have you seen our cat?" was written in big black letters below Tuffy's description. Then there was a whole series of posters announcing "REWARD! FOR LOST CAT!" And after putting our phone number on each sign, they set off to place them strategically throughout the neighborhood. To tell the truth, I was a little disappointed in their reaction. They seemed to be enjoying the challenge of finding Tuffy instead of grieving over her loss. But it was how they had chosen to handle the situation, and no matter how many times I told them it was hopeless, they refused to listen.

It wasn't until Amy was in bed that night that it hit her. I comforted her as best I could, but in the end she cried herself to sleep. Slipping quietly into her room later that night, I noticed a slip of paper up on her window that I hadn't seen before. Reading backwards through the paper, for it faced out toward the night, I read, "Tuffy come home. I love you." It was signed "Amy H." Tears sprang to my eyes so suddenly that I had to feel my way to the door.

For three days a shadow of gloom lay across the house. Then on the night of the third day Tuffy came home, making it a grand total of ten days missing. She came scratching on my bedroom window in the dead of night, but I knew instinctively it was Tuffy. Leaping out of bed, I switched on the light and said, "Jerry! Jerry! It's Tuffy!"

Even groggy with sleep he managed to come up with something clever. "Are you sure?" he asked. "It might be some cat who saw the posters and is impersonating Tuffy for the reward money."

Oh, what a joyful reunion it was the following morning. Amy said she knew all along Tuffy'd come back, and I said I'd never known an animal to return like that. It was our own Christmas miracle. It occurred to me later, though, that had I waited three more days before telling Amy and Katie about Tuffy's disappearance, they would never have known the difference. They would have been spared the agony of those three days, but they also would have been denied the thrill of her return. So in answer to Jerry's question I said, "Some things are worth taking risks for. And I'm sure Katie would agree."

"Why Katie?"

"Because, Jerry, *she's* the real animal lover in the family. Anyone who can cradle a twelve-inch lizard in her arms has it bad. She catches anything she can get her hands on and loves it and cares for it, until I release it after she goes to bed, that is. But she needs something that can love her back," I said.

"Well, what's wrong with Tuffy?"

"Tuffy's a cat," I said, feeling this was explanation enough. But seeing the blank look on his face, I sighed and tried to make myself clear. "Cats are independent creatures. Any animal that can come and go as it pleases, an outside cat like Tuffy, is bound to have a life beyond its people family. Are you following all this?" I stopped to ask.

"Every word," he answered, rummaging around in the refrigerator. "What happened to all that apple crisp we had last night?"

"Look behind the milk," I answered and then continued, "Anyway, it's hard to get to know a cat. They have subtle ways, and they don't tolerate a lot of silliness as they get older. Katie and Tuffy just never hit it off. She was only three and a half when we got Tuffy and couldn't understand why Tuffy didn't like being dressed in doll clothes and forced to ride in a buggy. Tuffy stays clear of Katie because she never knows when Katie may make her dance on her hind legs. And when Tuffy scratches her to get away, it hurts Katie's feelings," I paused thinking about how pathetic Katie always looked after one of Tuffy's rebukes.

"Well, sometimes she deserves it," Jerry remarked. "She should learn to respect Tuffy's integrity. Amy does."

"I know. That's why *they're* so close. Amy's more of a cat person. She understands Tuffy, and so Tuffy feels more comfortable with Amy. She's much more Amy's cat than Katie's. Do you remember what Katie said after Tuffy returned from the dead that time?"

"No. What was it?"

"She said, 'Does this mean we won't be getting a new kitten?' I had said that if Tuffy didn't come back we would," I filled him in.

"Well, she's never felt the same about Tuffy ever since she got hold of her first rat," Jerry commented.

"Oh, poor kid. That was so awful!" I answered. It had happened about a year ago. We gave Katie a darling baby rat for her fourth birthday. Having given Amy her first rat at that age, we discovered them to be dandy pets, regardless of how the more finicky mothers felt. Katie had been delighted with her furry friend and carried it with her everywhere. Despite repeated warnings, she didn't really believe Tuffy would harm "Randy." Such is the innocence of a four-year-old. One evening she came prancing down the stairs with Randy riding in a birthday hat, which, when carried by its rubber chin strap, made a convenient cone-shaped carryall. Katie waltzed over to where Tuffy was sleeping peacefully on the rocking chair and offered her a glimpse of Randy with a wave of her hand. One yellow eye opened to a slit and then closed again. Satisfied that Tuffy was in no way interested, Katie removed Randy from the hat, placing him on the floor in front of her. Before any of us could say anything, Tuffy had made her move. Grabbing Katie, I smothered her face against my chest to block the scene from her sight and screamed for Jerry to "do something." He did, and what it was I never asked. Even though it was a painful episode and I worried about the long-term effect it would have on her, it was an older and wiser Katie that entered the pet store later that week. Marching up to the rat cages, she announced, "This time I want a bigger one." She learned her lesson the hard way, and you can be sure that it wasn't one she'd soon forget. Randy II's rides in the Barbie motorhome and trips in the circus train were now confined to Katie's room, a towel wedged into the crack under the door. Only after a thorough search of the house to determine Tuffy's whereabouts did Randy II venture beyond the safety of her room—and only then in the green plastic picnic basket. So, as much as I hate to say it, perhaps it was for the best. We all have to grow up sometime.

Picking up the conversation again, I added, "And every time Katie rescues a lizard from Tuffy's clutches or warns a bird of an impending attack, they grow further and further apart."

"Oh, Julie, you make it sound so dramatic," Jerry scoffed.

"Well, it's important. Katie needs an outlet, an understanding companion. Remember her teddy bear? At least this time she'd be talking to something alive!"

"She's too young to handle the responsibility. Who do you think will *really* take care of it? Not me, you can be sure of that."

Past the "over my dead body" stage, we had progressed to discussion. It wouldn't be long before we moved to the bargaining table. But these final stages were crucial and I had to be very careful not to blow the whole deal.

So I said casually, "Well, that's another reason it would be good for Katie; she needs more responsibility." And then, before he could answer, I added, "But I don't want to make you mad. Let's not talk about it anymore right now."

This was an important move because it gave the impression that I had given in, putting him in a generous frame of mind, so that when I added, "Just think about it, okay?" he said, "I'll *think* about it, but that's *all* I'll do." Not exactly a victory, but a beginning.

And while he was thinking about it, I would be gathering data for the next phase in the great dog debate.

What the Books Said

Falling somewhere after "Pediatrician" and just before "Play," "Pets" was one of the easiest problems I've had to research in a long time. I turned to *The Mother's Almanac* first, feeling they'd be more sympathetic to my cause than some of the others. And sure enough, "Pets" actually came as a subtitle under the grander category RESPONSIBILITY. "A child must learn to be responsible for four things, his toys, his clothes, his pets and himself . . . the Five who can clean his hamster cage alone or the Six who can pick up most of his toys will be a self-confident child and proud to have earned the respect that comes with his accomplishments." Oh, Jerry will go for that. And listen to this: "Even with the best of care, a pet usually has a rather short life expectancy, but his death, although tragic, is still a child's most gentle introduction to the natural cycle. The sorrow of death can never be greater than the gift of life." Gee, that made me feel better about Randy I—the part about "the natural cycle" being the most appropriate. Following this general discussion of pets came a list of recommended pets. Ants came up, reminding me of the ant farm we bought for Amy when she was six. The kit came with a coupon to mail away for several dozen giant black ants. The tunnels they carved out of the lightweight sand, also supplied with the kit, were fascinating, but soon over half the population had died off. It could have been for any number of reasons, not the least of them being the avalanches Katie would inflict upon this poor struggling civilization as she was "studying" them. Soon there was only a lone survivor, tirelessly carrying dead bodies to the burial grounds. It seemed so cruel that I finally dumped the whole mess into the garden. Later I worried that this one giant ant might breed with others, creating a new strain, and visions of giant ants marching to avenge their dead brothers and sisters haunted me for weeks.

Gerbils, turtles, and rabbits were then discussed, and about guinea pigs Kelly and Parsons said, "A guinea pig can soak up as much affection as your Five cares to give. There is little else this dear animal can be except a terrific cuddle figure."

Snakes was the next section up, but, having been that route, I only bothered reading the part about "lodgings," curious as to why *our* snakes were always able to slip out of their cages. I learned that "Because a snake is almost solid muscle, he can push the top from any cage if it isn't heavy enough." Solid muscle, huh? Well, that explains it. Once, when we had gone on vacation, my mother was put in charge of feeding "Red Specks," as Amy had appropriately named her snake. Upon our return Red Specks's cage was suspiciously empty. My mother swore up one side and down the other that she had, not once but *twice,* scooped him up (with bare hands, she had emphasized) and returned him to his cage. Even after I took her aside and explained that I wouldn't blame her a bit if she hadn't *really* retrieved the snake, she stuck to her story. "You can tell *me,* Mom," I had said, but she just shook her head and repeated, "Not once, but *twice.*" We spent a nerve-racking week wondering where he'd turn up before Jerry finally found him in the shower one morning.

But enough of this; what about the dog? "Even a smart puppy requires a lot of time," the authors began. "The younger the dog the more trouble he'll cause, since a puppy goes through stages just like a child. . . . House training will be your biggest problem . . ." and so on. Gee, this made a dog sound like an awful lot of work. What was that they said about guinea pigs?

In Joan Beck's chapter "Child-Pet Problems" (not a promising title) she deferred to Dr. Boris Levinson, an expert on people-pet relationships, on the question "What kind of pet is best for a child?" He answered, "Whatever the youngster has been asking for—provided it doesn't cause more inconvenience than you can tolerate." And he further advised, "Before you get any pet, work through your own feelings about animals, decide how much time you can spare for pet care and discuss the choice thoroughly in a family conference." Oops, the family conference isn't until phase four.

I found some fascinating, if not bizarre, stories in the "Pets and Other Animals" section of *Kids: Day In and Day Out.* Harvey Jacobs told how he was able to put off buying his son, four and a half, a dog by pretending to be a horse. And further on was a letter written to Dear Abby by a father who was mad at himself because "I let an 8-year-old con-artist talk me into buying him a dog!" It was signed "Growling Mad."

I flipped past "How to Catch Flies for Your Frog," "So You Want to Import a Pet," and "Chickens I Have Known," looking for verification that a dog was, in fact, the right way to go. I didn't find it. But before moving on, I read "The Death of a Pet," a short narrative by Selma Fraiberg (author of *The Magic Years)* in which a mother worried about what to tell her five-year-old son when she discovers his hamster has died. It caught my immediate attention, having had a similar experience when Amy's first rat (Lori I) died. I remember seeing that stiff form lying still in the cage and knowing instinctively she was a goner. Jerry had already left for work, so I had no one with whom to counsel. The big question seemed to be, Do I tell her now, or wait for her to go off to kindergarten, using that time to discreetly dispose of Lori and come up with a plausible story? Thinking back to the various pets I had mourned as a child, I felt it would be wrong to arbitrarily deny her the experience. Pressing my fingernails into the palms of my hands, a trick I use to prevent myself from crying, I said, "Amy, I think Lori is dead."

"What? Let me see." Amy opened the cage and gave

Lori a few pokes. No response. "Yeah, you're right. I wonder why?" she asked as she stared uncertainly at the rat.

"Why?" I repeated. It wasn't what I had expected, although it made perfectly good sense. "Old age, I imagine," I said.

"I'm glad I played with her yesterday," Amy said thoughtfully. "She rode in the townhouse elevator and everything."

That's probably what did it, I thought to myself; one ride too many in Barbie's pink elevator, hurtling down the three flights of cardboard townhouse, only to come to a crashing stop on the patio. And then the image of that small whiskered face peeking out from inside the Fisher-Price school bus got to me and I ran to the bathroom, unable to control my tears.

"Mom? Are you okay?" Amy called after me.

"It's just that she was such a good f-f-friend," I stammered, trying to pull myself together.

"Yeah, I'm going to miss her," Amy said quietly. And then as an afterthought she added, "What'll we do with her?" Practical, that's Amy for you.

"Well, we could bury her and have a little funeral for her," I suggested, wiping my eyes.

"How do you do that?" she asked.

And as I explained about funerals, burials, and graveyards, it occurred to me that this was her first experience with death. Since she'd have to come to terms with it sooner or later, maybe it was better to introduce the concept now. A funeral appealed to her sense of order, and we gently transferred Lori from her cage (a job only for the hardy, and even then a lot of tissues are recommended) into a shoe box lined with cotton balls. Funeral services, postponed until after school, were held in the backyard with only the immediate family attending.

And, according to Selma Fraiberg, that was the right thing

to do. "We need to respect a child's right to experience a loss fully and deeply. . . . What right do we have to deprive children their feelings? Why aren't they entitled to their grief over the death of a pet?" And don't forget mothers! We're entitled to grief too, you know!

And about buying a new pet, she says, "The time for replacing the lost pet is when mourning has done its work and the child himself is ready to attach himself to a new animal." Our rats usually lasted a couple of years before taking that last elevator ride to the top or the final spin around the race track in the battery-operated sports car. Lori I being the first in a long line of rats, we did indeed learn to let the grieving child determine when it was time to buy a new one, a respectable mourning lasting anywhere from two to four months.

But, getting back on the right track, I turned to Spock in a final attempt to find support for my campaign. There was no listing for pets, which would have fallen between "Pertussis, see Whooping cough" and "Pharyngitis, see Sore throat," so I tried under "Dog.". . . "Diseases," "Doctor," "Dog bites". . . but no "Dog." Oh, well, perhaps Maggie could give me some ideas.

What Maggie Said

"Tom's been talking about getting the kids a dog," Maggie informed me when I spoke to her later that day. "But I'm against it."

"Why?"

"Oh, Julie, they're so much work. I have my hands full as it is without a puppy complicating things."

"Yeah, they do require a lot of care at first," I answered,

thinking about all I had read about teething, housebreaking, diet, and shots.

"Not just at first, Julie—*forever*," Maggie emphasized.

"Did *you* ever have a dog?" I asked Maggie. "I mean as a child."

"No, my father had allergies," Maggie answered.

"Oh, Maggie, that's the oldest trick in the book!" I laughed. "Tell me, when was your father's last big attack?"

"I don't know. He doesn't get them anymore," Maggie said thoughtfully.

"My parents once told me I was allergic to bird feathers and I had to give away my parakeet. I went around for years telling people I was allergic to birds, writing it down on medical questionnaires, avoiding aviaries at the zoo, I didn't learn the truth for years until my mother finally broke down and told me that the bird was a nuisance and they wanted an excuse to get rid of it."

"Well, I think my dad really did have allergies," said Maggie, not wanting to look the fool after all these years.

"Perhaps, but I'll bet that nine out of ten kids who *don't* have dogs will tell you they have a parent who's allergic to dog hair." And then, returning to my original question, I said, "Well, *I* had a dog, several actually, and some of my happiest memories are wrapped up in them. I was the only girl with brothers on either side of me, remember—"

"Ooh, a *middle* child!" Maggie interjected.

"That's right!" I laughed. "And those dogs were special to me. But as the oldest of five kids, you were too busy being an overachiever to worry about dogs, right?" I teased.

"Too busy baby-sitting, anyway," Maggie answered. "My brothers and sister, those were my pets!"

"I guess it's just that, like Katie, I'm a real animal lover at heart. But I don't want to do something foolish that I'll live to regret. A parakeet is one thing, but you can't renege on a dog quite as easily."

"You know, you're the one who I think wants the dog," Maggie said. She always could see right through me.

"Well, I suppose there's some truth to that."

"There's nothing wrong with getting a dog," Maggie encouraged. "Just don't pretend it's only for the kids."

She was absolutely right. I could see it now: torn newspapers all over the house and me ranting, "We get the dog you want so badly and then you don't even take care of it!" An ugly scene that fortunately Maggie's perspective enabled her to foretell, my own Ghost of Puppy Future, if you will. And not unlike Scrooge, I got the message. "I see what you mean, Maggie, and you're right. Thanks for the advice."

"Anytime, you know that." And I did.

What My Mother Said

"I don't know why you didn't think of it sooner," my mother said when I asked her what she thought of our getting a dog. Amy, Katie, and I had been on our way out the door for a walk around the neighborhood when my mother stopped by. She decided to join us, and as the girls skipped on ahead we continued our conversation.

"Don't say anything to them," I said, indicating Amy and Katie, who were crouched behind a bush up ahead of us, presumably preparing an attack. "Jerry hasn't agreed to anything yet, and I'm not a hundred percent sure myself."

"Oh, but just think how thrilled they would be. Especially Katie," my mother said dreamily.

"I know, and Amy's so responsible I'm sure she'd be a big help." Just then the girls sprang out from their hiding place onto the sidewalk in front of us. We threw our hands in the air and screamed in feigned fright. Thoroughly pleased with what they believed to be a successful surprise, they dashed off to plan a fresh attack.

My mother laughed to herself and said thoughtfully, "Yes, a dog would be nice; a lot of work, mind you, but worth it. A dog can reciprocate a child's love, whereas other animals aren't as expressive. I mean, how much feedback can you really get from a rat?"

"Oh, I don't know, whiskers can be pretty expressive!"

"Well, I think the children would learn a lot from having a dog, to say nothing of helping Katie express her feelings."

"My sentiments exactly," I answered, pleased to have finally found someone to verify my original theory.

And at that moment we were suddenly set upon by two wild beasts who, jumping out from behind a parked car, really did scare us that time.

What My Husband Said

Interestingly enough, it was Jerry who brought up the subject again. It was a beautiful Saturday morning, and we had decided to picnic at the country park located in the hills behind our house. Coming into the kitchen with the cooler from the garage, he said, "I've been thinking about what you said about getting a dog."

"Oh?"

"Maybe I was a little hasty in my decision. I was really just thinking of myself and the hassle a dog would be to me, without considering what it would mean to the girls. I forget sometimes to see things from a kid's point of view, you know." His admission took me by surprise. These kinds of confessions didn't come easily for Jerry, and for some silly reason I always felt grateful when he shared them with me.

"That's true," I agreed because, in fact, it was. He was always pointing out the sleazy side of carnivals or the overpriced cost of a cheap thrill. "But the kids don't see the bums behind the booths, or understand that eight dollars is too much to pay to see the Trees of Mystery," I would argue. But *he* did, and that was enough. Then again, he had his softer moments, and this was one of them.

"But we love you anyway," I added, reaching up to wrap my arms around his neck and plant a kiss on his Saturday-morning beard.

"Yeah, me too," he answered, blushing slightly.

"But now *I'm* not so sure that a dog is such a good idea." And I was almost as surprised as he was at my comment.

"Really? Why not?"

"Well, for one thing, I think it was more for me than the kids. . . . And you thought *you* were selfish!" He laughed and I continued, "And looking into it reminded me of just how much work a dog really is. There are alternatives, for the time being, anyway."

"Well, like what?" I could tell he was relieved to be off the hook but didn't want to act too pleased.

"Oh, guinea pigs or rabbits. Both very cuddly if you treat them right."

"Okay, talk to the girls and see what they think. We can go over to the pet store this weekend and check it out." Oh, but he was in a generous mood now. I tried to think of something I could ask for. Dinner out? A movie, maybe? C'mon, Julie, think big—a weekend in Palm Springs. How much is *not* having to get a dog worth, anyway?

What I Did

It was more like what *we* did. First we talked about pets. I guess you could have called it a "family conference." We discussed those pets we thought were the cutest or cleanest or that had the most personality. And we all agreed that we were tired of rats. Then it was off to the pet store to see if they had an animal that met the minimum requirements of cuddly, quiet, cheap to feed (Jerry's), and willing to ride in a doll buggy (Katie's). We decided on a guinea pig. We chose a long-haired female whose fur spiraled into multicolored cowlicks. Katie giggled helplessly as it squirmed in her arms. Laughter being as contagious as it is, we were all tittering foolishly as we passed the lively ball of fur from one to the other.

As soon as we got home, Amy made out a rotating schedule, allowing the guinea pig a week in each room. This seemed like a fair arrangement and broke up the responsibility into workable units. The only thing left, then, was the name. Katie voted for Lori, but Amy put her foot down, declaring enough was enough. A long list of names ensued, some finding their origins in food, like Taffy, Cream Puff, and Butterscotch, while others were based on action—from Scamper to Sleepy. We finally narrowed it down to either Molly or Butterscotch. And it was Katie who suggested we combine the names and call her Butterscotch Molly. It had a nice ring to it—kind of like Calamity Jane—and so it stuck.

My mother was thrilled and fully agreed that a dog would be more than we bargained for just now. She always did that—took a firm stand on an idea she thought I was in favor of and then, when I changed my mind, she'd say, "I never did like that idea in the first place!" I pointed this out to her, and she said, "That's because I only want what you want." Spoken like a true mother.

And in case you're wondering, *not* having to get a dog wasn't worth a weekend away, but it did get me dinner and a movie!

9

A Solution to Santa
or
The Crisis at
Christmas

"Mommy! Look!" Katie cried out as we pulled into the supermarket parking lot. "Christmas decorations!"

"Where?" I asked unbelievingly. We had just packed away the Halloween costumes, and I still had sores on my tongue from eating all of Katie's trick-or-treat candy.

"On the lamps," Katie said, pointing to the big cement pillars situated throughout the parking lot.

"Oh, yeah," I answered slowly, still trying to adjust to the idea of Christmas being just around the corner. If I didn't know better, I'd swear it was coming earlier every year.

Amy, Katie, and I sat in the car admiring the boughs of shimmering tinsel that wound their way up the lampposts and the silver bells that swayed in the breeze at the top.

"When can we get our tree?" Amy asked dreamily.

"Oh, honey, it's way too early to be thinking about a Christmas tree!" I said gently. "The decorations are just up to help everyone get into the holiday mood." I shifted uneasily in my seat, thinking about the upcoming holidays. I had a hard time resisting seasonal advertising. Last August I went out in ninety-degree heat and bought Amy two wool skirts and a jumper just because I had seen a big Back-to-School apple hanging in the drugstore window. And in May and June I have a terrible time with all the plastic pools, snorkle sets, and sand toys that fit together to resemble a treasure chest (not that you can ever get them to go back like that once they're apart) that are being promoted that time of the year. So you can imagine what it's like for me at Christmas. And every year I tell myself the same thing: "Don't overdo. Don't get carried away." But every year I do anyway. Parked under those silver bells sparkling in the November sun, I silently renewed my Christmas vows.

Inside, the market had been completely done over in preparation for the coming holidays. Cans of black olives, boxes of stuffing mix, and jars of maraschino cherries were stacked at the end of each aisle, and where last week's ghost had hung, there was a snowman, corncob pipe and all. We worked our way from one end of the store to the other, sticking strictly to our list, but turning down the pet-food aisle we discovered it entirely reorganized to accommodate an additional toy section. The usual crayons, coloring books, and plastic bags of army men had been replaced by the more trendy He Man action figures, Ewoks, and Smurf villages.

"Oh! They have Rough Riders!" Amy exclaimed and then begged, "Please, Mom?"

But before I could answer, there was a squeal of delight from Katie, who had discovered the Shirt Tail train set.

"Put all that stuff back," I said firmly, and, grabbing up three cans of cat food, I made a dash for the dairy department. But there was no escaping Christmas's impending approach. Cartons of eggnog lined the refrigerated shelves, and both Amy and Katie were sure that they loved this "Christmas drink."

"Your father likes it, anyway," I said as I hoisted a half-gallon into the cart.

Jingle bells, jingle bells . . .

Standing in the checkout line, I studied the magazine rack in front of me. The holiday issues had just hit the stands, and I gazed wistfully at dining rooms in which candlelight reflected off crystal goblets, eight-foot Christmas trees decorated entirely from hand-crafted ornaments, and country kitchens filled to overflowing with pastries from around the world. It wouldn't surprise me a bit if the covers of *McCalls*, *Good Housekeeping*, and *Ladies' Home Journal* were found to be responsible for a great number of Christmas nervous breakdowns. I mean, no matter how hard I might try, my dining room could never look like that—it's all done with mirrors anyway—but that isn't to say I don't want it to. *Au contraire.* Last year I attempted to duplicate a page from the Home section of the *Los Angeles Times*. I strung tiny white lights throughout the house to give it that fairyland effect. There *was* a problem in finding outlets to accommodate all the cords running behind couches and under tables, and while I won't bore you with the extension-cord stories, let me just say that the clerk down at the hardware store and I are now on a first-name basis. The attainment of this dream was not without its sacrifices, however. Choices had to be made. Did we want to enjoy the ultimate in Christmas fantasy, or did we want to turn on the lamps and watch television? You couldn't have it both ways, and one evening as we sat surrounded by twinkling lights Jerry asked, "How much longer do you think we'll be in this wonderland tonight? U.S.C. kicks off in fifteen minutes." I guess it all depends on your definition of spirit.

So I tried to keep things in perspective as I considered this year's holiday suggestions. Apparently it was the year of the craft. There wasn't magazine to be seen that didn't proclaim to hold within its covers a treasury of easy-to-make gifts and decorations. There was everything from holiday characters you could cut out and color to unique gifts made out of upholstery webbing (oh, good, I've been wondering what to do with all my extra upholstery webbing!). Life-sized boots as Christmas stockings sounded bizarre enough as it was, but when I read "Decorate-A-Dinette," printed in bold red letters, I could no longer supress my laughter.

"What's so funny, Mom?" Amy stopped fondling the candy bars long enough to ask.

"Oh, just something I read in one of these magazines," I explained, still chuckling to myself.

She followed my gaze to the magazine rack and exclaimed, "Oh! Look at that cute Santa Claus decoration! Can we make one for our door?"

A fresh spasm of laughter passed through my body before I noticed the brightness of her eyes and the excitement in her voice. I took a second look at the Santa doll. Well, it didn't look all that hard, really. And, after all, who is Christmas for, if not the kids? I reached out and pulled the magazine from the rack. "We can *try,* anyway," I said, smiling.

Amy clapped her hands in joy and called to her sister, who was hanging upside down on the chrome bars behind the register, "Katie! We get to make a Santa for our door!"

Katie's face lit up as she jumped down from the bar. "Oh, boy!" Then she and Amy did a little dance just beyond the checkout stand by the big bags of charcoal and kitty litter.

Frosty the snowman was a jolly, happy soul. . . .

Back at home we sat around the kitchen table sipping eggnog that the children swore up one side and down the other that they liked, though they hardly touched it, and seriously studied the Santa project. "Saint Nick" would require one six-inch-diameter "plastic-foam ball" (does that mean plastic *or* foam, or is there some new kind of material that is actually called plastic-foam?); felt; yarn; bristol board (is that plywood? tagboard? cardboard?); wooden beads; thread; scissors; straight pins; double-faced masking tape (now, that one I knew); glue; a large bread knife with serrated blade; more thread, this time heavy duty; spray Accent transparent paint (what? Is Accent a brand name? Will the clerk at the hardware store still remember my name? I already hated this project); marking pens, brown wrapping paper; and red and blue acrylic paints.

I read through the list of materials again, this time out loud to Amy and Katie.

"That's an awful lot of stuff," Amy commented in the silence that followed.

"I'm wondering," I began slowly, "if perhaps some other project might be simpler." A small square of graph paper at the bottom of the page had caught my eye. Step 2 of Saint Nick read, "Enlarge diagram for layered beard and mustache on brown wrapping paper." I had tried to enlarge a bunny pattern once for a pair of slippers. I remember its being rather difficult and when Amy, for whom the slippers were intended, saw them she thought they were mice. "Here's a whole page of decorations you can make from cat-food cans," I added, pushing the magazine over in their direction.

"Let's make Christmas tree ornaments!" Amy suggested, pointing to a display of ornaments made from plastic six-pack holders and used flash cubes. Fine, I thought to myself, we can always hang them at the back of the tree. And as long as I didn't have to hunt down plastic-foam or bristol board, I didn't care what they decided to make.

Katie continued to study the magazine, finding even more possibilities for food jars, Q-tips, and margarine tubs. Amy, on the other hand, went off to make out her Christmas list.

I got up and began to rinse off the lunch dishes. Outside the kitchen window a hummingbird was darting from bush to bush. Christmas seemed light years away. But I knew from experience that it had a way of sneaking up on you, and this year I wasn't going to be taken by surprise. My goal was to have all my shopping done by December seventh, tenth at the latest. In fact, that is *always* my goal. But I inevitably become bogged down searching for the doll that's on back order or the toy that's been discontinued. And if I am so lucky as to find the elusive item in some all-night drugstore forty miles away, it never fails but that it has been scratched from the Christmas list by then, replaced by whatever is being currently advertised on television. Indeed, television commercials probably are the number-two cause of stress at Christmas (number one being the don't-you-wish-your-house-looked-like-this magazine covers, of course). Last December, when Katie watched her Saturday-morning cartoons, she would cry out, "I want it!" every time they advertised some hideous life-sized doll or race track that ran halfway up the wall. At four years old the true meaning of Christmas still hadn't sunk in, and she couldn't understand why I always marched over and snapped off the television in disgust after about the fourth outburst. Thinking of this, I called to Amy to come down so we could discuss this Christmas-list business.

"First of all," I began, "the Christmas tradition is really about giving, not receiving gifts—like the Wise Men bringing gifts to Jesus." Both girls stared at me with blank looks on their faces. I knew they were preparing themselves for my Christmas-is-a-time-for-giving lecture. I decided to hold off on it. No point in going into all that until later, when I had a more receptive audience. Like the coal-in-the-stocking routine, I wanted to be careful not to use it too early in the season. Children are notoriously naughty around Christmastime—all that excitement you know, not to mention the pressure of Santa watching every move they make. (Hey, I wouldn't want to carry that around with me all day.) So it's important to begin with just your basic reminder not to be selfish or greedy and work up to the declaration that anything purchased so far *is* returnable. The more drastic measure of announcing, "If you think Santa is going to bring a child who refuses to wash her hair a Merry-Go-Round Stroller, guess again!" will hopefully buy some time so that the phone call to the North Pole can be avoided altogether. If not, though, it's important to remember to speak only to the Chief Elf and not Santa himself. This allows some flexibility in case "Santa" should bring the gift in question after all. A "breakdown in communications" will explain this error as well as convince a child of Santa's autonomy from parental pressure. The Christmas Amy was six and a half and finding inconsistencies in the Santa story line, she discovered nail polish in her stocking Christmas morning. Knowing my aversion to nail polish on children, she could only assume that there really was a Santa Claus. It was, however, a bittersweet kind of victory. The deception was so complete that I worried about the inevitable day when she found out the truth. How far should the con really go? was the question. The recollection made me uneasy because I had yet to resolve this complex issue. Amy would be eight this Christmas, and she still believed in Santa Claus. But I wondered if we'd get away with it this year. . . . I wondered if, in fact, we should even try.

Picking the conversation back up, I continued, "You should really be jotting down ideas of what *others* might like for Christmas." And then, just as a test, I added, "Instead of worrying about what to ask Santa to bring you." Amy didn't bat an eye, and so I decided to cross that bridge when I came to it.

By the time Thanksgiving had come and gone we had managed to save more cans, jars, six-pack holders, and flash cubes than you'd care to imagine. Amy and Katie had decided to make enough ornaments to give away as gifts to aunts, uncles, grandmas, and grandpas this year. As thrilled as I was by their enthusiasm to make presents, I was less than thrilled by the results of their efforts. Sprayed gold and sprinkled with glitter, the six-pack holders looked like exotic snakes twisting around in some grotesque mating ritual. The flash-cube ornaments weren't much better. Sprayed a bright fluorescent pink (don't ask me why, it's what the magazine suggested) and glued together, they looked more like Barbie robots than any Christmas-tree ornament I'd ever seen. But Amy and Katie thought they were dandy and were having a hard time deciding which ones to give away.

Because their Christmas lists had been rewritten so many times (commercials being longer and more entertaining than the shows they're sponsoring this time of year), I hadn't been able to do much shopping for the kids. I had, however, found an asparagus steamer for my mother, a recording of Verdi's *Othello* for my father, and the seat covers for Jerry's truck he'd been looking for. This year I was sure to surprise him. It'd been weeks since he'd last discussed the covers, and I had listened in my usual uninterested way. I couldn't wait to see the look on his face. And he wasn't going to get it out of me, either. Every year he guessed his present the week before Christmas and then ended up opening it early since he already knew what it was. He also tries to get me to guess what my present is from him. When I refuse, he gives me hints anyway. He's worse than the children. My mother-in-law was another story. It was hard to find just the right gift for her. But I had seen these electric slippers in a catalogue that would be perfect. Her house gets quite cold at night, and she likes to stay up late watching television. Electric slippers would be ideal. It was, of course, too late to order them from the catalogue, but I felt confident that I could find a pair somewhere. I'd call around.

Meanwhile I roamed the malls looking for "something small" for various brothers and sisters and endless nieces and nephews. Walking past the fabric store one day, I stopped to admire the array of Christmas crafts in the display window. Caught up in the festive fever that emits from that much green and red felt all in one place, I decided to make Amy and Katie matching nightgowns for Christmas Eve. Half an hour later I emerged from the store laden with several yards of red flannel, matching thread, and the white eyelet lace that would make the nightgowns picture-perfect.

Two weeks later the kids were out of school and the red flannel still lay in a bag on the floor of my closet. I hadn't been able to locate Helen's electric slippers yet (and asking for them was becoming increasingly embarrassing), and Amy and Katie, having run out of plastic six-pack rings, had graduated to the Moroccan candlesticks, which consisted of leftover food jars and glittered tape. We had yet to visit Santa in his workshop at the shopping center, decorate Christmas cookies, plan our annual neighborhood caroling party, and get our tree. How did this happen? I thought I had everything under control.

Oh, you better watch out, you better not cry. . . .

That night I went out shopping right after dinner, leaving Jerry to put the kids to bed. It was a last-ditch attempt to finish off my shopping. Dashing in and out of stores, I slowly worked my way down my list. I had decided to get Amy and Katie some nice books, a couple of records, new clothes, and a tetherball set. Nothing pink or plastic, nothing with more than four moving parts, and nothing that required assembly—the kids would probably be disappointed.

The following morning I felt a little guilty. "Let me just *see* your lists," I said after breakfast. Amy went off to gather together what she referred to as her "Christmas notebook." Oh, God.

Katie, on the other hand, shrugged her shoulders pathetically and said, "I don't have a list because I don't know what all there is to get."

"Oh, Katie!" I said, giving her a big hug. "You're so funny!"

"And I don't know how to spell," she added sheepishly, admitting what was probably the real reason.

When Amy returned with her spiral-bound notebook, I was all ready with my there-are-some-children-who-feel-lucky-to-get-a-penny-in-their-stocking lecture (the second in the four-part True Meaning of Christmas series). But on the first page I read:

WHAT MOM WANTS

1. Slippers
2. A knife that cuts
3. Peace and quiet [spelled *pese* and *kwit* . . . same thing]

WHAT DAD WANTS

1. A new car
2. A longer hose
3. Socks that match

WHAT KATIE WANTS

1. Whatever I get

"Oh, Amy," I said softly, not trusting my voice. "This is so nice." I didn't really know what else to say. I had been prepared to chastise her for her greediness and instead I was the one who felt humbled.

"Well, you said to jot down ideas," Amy explained, and then she cracked her famous smile and added, "And you're *always* asking for peace and quiet, so I put it down!" Katie and I cracked up.

"Did you make a list for yourself?" I asked, a little worried. Too much goody-goody could mean she was coming down with something.

"Turn the page," Amy answered.

There in neat letters she had listed:

Kimberly Cheerleader doll
Shirt Tails radio and headset
Tetherball
Watch
Skates

"This looks like a reasonable list of things for Santa to choose from. Don't you have a watch?"

"I can't find it," she answered and then asked quickly, "What do you mean, 'to choose from'? How do you know he can't bring them all?"

"Well, that would be too much."

"Why? He doesn't have to pay for the presents," she persisted.

"No, but the elves have to make it all, and if every boy and girl received ten presents they'd never get it all done—not to mention how they'd deliver all those gifts. Santa chooses those things he thinks you'll enjoy the most or those that he has enough of. Sometimes he runs out of certain toys, doesn't realize their popularity, and then he brings something else instead." I was about to explain how tough it was for Santa to fill all these orders without the benefit of a presale, but the look on Amy's face stopped me. "What is it, honey?" I asked, already knowing the answer.

"Is there really a Santa Claus?"

I looked into those troubled blue eyes and said the only thing that came to mind, "What do you think?"

"I don't know."

"What made you ask, then?" I wanted to know where I stood before committing myself one way or another.

"I don't know," she insisted. "I just wondered, that's all."

"Well, let's not talk about it in front of Katie. We might upset her." Changing the subject I asked, "What do you say we get started on the tin-can ornaments today?"

"Yeah!" said Katie, all smiles.

"Okay," Amy answered thoughtfully. And I knew that I didn't have long to find the answers to some pretty tough questions.

What the Books Said

It turned out that the first step in making our "perforated cylinders" was to fill the juice cans with water and freeze them so that when we began punching patterns in them they wouldn't bend out of shape. Pretty clever, huh? I had never have thought of that on my own and could only imagine the crumpled mess I'd have had on my hands, had I not read the directions. But that meant we couldn't really begin the project for a couple of hours. So while Amy and Katie roller-skated out front, I decided to see what the experts had to say about the Santa Claus mystique.

In *The Mother's Almanac* the subject was listed simply as "Santa Claus." And while there was the obvious advice to tell children beforehand that all the Santas they see in department stores are only helpers, and to let them prepare Santa a snack on Christmas Eve to assuage any last-minute doubts about being "good," there was nothing concrete about what and when to tell a child the truth about Santa. What they did say was, "A child will believe in elves (and bunny rabbits and the tooth fairy) if he needs to believe and as long as it makes him happy to believe. No matter when a child accepts the truth, he always is wise enough to recognize the Santa Claus story for what it is—another guise of your love." I wondered. . . .

Santa Claus was not listed in Dr. Spock's *Baby and Child Care* index, which went from "Sandwiches" to "Scabies" (I couldn't resist looking this up, and they turned out to be just what I thought: "groups of pimples topped with scabs and . . ." Heard enough?). And Christmas was a dead end, too.

Ask Dr. Salk, however, had listed "The Truth About Santa Claus" as one of his parent questions. This was preceded by "Children's 'Greediness' at Christmas" and followed by "Christmas and the Disappointed Child." I settled down for some serious reading. "I'm not at all against perpetuating the *myth* of Santa," began Dr. Salk. "I'm opposed to telling children that Santa Claus is real"— uh-oh—"and then building on this basic untruth, most parents compound the problem even further by continuing to lie about how Santa can get around to so many places in such a short time or what happens if a house has no chimney." Not to mention how it happens that he uses the same wrapping paper you do or that sometimes his toys are "Made in Japan." "Ultimately," Dr. Salk continues, "when a child learns the truth, trust in his or her parents can be seriously undermined." Wow, this was a far cry from "recognizing the story as another guise of your love." I read on about how children were able to enjoy fantasies, but the bottom line was, "Children should be told the truth about Santa Claus when they ask if he is real." Amy's troubled question came back into my mind, and I still wondered how I would answer her.

"Christmas and the Disappointed Child" turned out to be about a mother who didn't know how to tell her eight-year-old daughter that no way was she getting the three-hundred-dollar dollhouse in the toy store window for Christmas. Again, Salk advised to go with the truth. And in "Children's 'Greediness' at Christmas," Dr. Salk said that children listing endless toys that they've seen and want does not represent greediness but is "a reaction to the excitement, the indulgence, and the departure from the constraints that adults attempt to exercise throughout the rest of the year." Well, this, at least, made me feel better. But he went on to say that it was only natural for children to make endless requests for gifts when they felt it came from a workshop loaded to the brim. And he also pointed out that not receiving a toy specifically asked for could be seen as an indication of their "badness"; all the more reason to let children know that *real* people are the ones who give the presents. This reminded me of my absurd explanation to Amy of why she couldn't have all the toys of her list. What was it I had said? Something about elves working their fingers to the bone? Oh, what a tangled web we weave. . . .

I passed on "Christmas in the Tropics" and "The Christmas Letdown" and turned to *Effective Parenting* for a third opinion. Under "Santa Claus, belief in," I found the advice that "the key to the situation is to so order your Christmas celebration that your child begins to appreciate its true significance long before he outgrows Santa Claus. Before he is six or seven, he can be helped to understand the religious faith that is the foundation of Christmas. He can sample the addictive joy of giving instead of getting, if you encourage him to make Christmas gifts for others. Children who are helped to become participants in the celebration of Christmas rather than just spectators rarely miss Santa Claus very much or for very long." Oh, I liked the sound of that. It sure beat the serious undermining of the child's trust in his parents that Salk had referred to.

Among her various strategies for coping with the Santa situation I found the "reverse parry" to be right up my alley. "To learn what a child wants to believe about Santa Claus, a parent can parry the 'Is there really a Santa?' question with a loving 'What do you think, honey?' If the youngster hopes to have his faith upheld, he'll probably reply something like 'Johnny just said that to tease me; I know there's a Santa because. . . .' But if a child is ready to give up the myth, he may answer, 'Oh, I knew it was made-up stuff for little kids all along.' A parent can then safely launch into a Yes-but-Virginia strategy." Of course, I hadn't been so fortunate as to have received such a clear-cut answer from Amy, but maybe next time she'd reveal her true feelings.

The problem with most of this advice, though, was that it really pertained to how the myth should be handled from the beginning. It was a little late for that now. I had already gone to a great deal of trouble explaining why the reindeer at the zoo didn't fly, as well as how it is that you can exchange a gift from Santa at a Sears department store. But the moment of truth was upon us, and for Amy, age eight, perhaps even overdue.

What Maggie Said

I had expected to find Maggie in a tizzy this close to Christmas, but I was wrong.

"Oh, I'm completely organized," she answered confidently when I asked how she was getting along.

"Really? I'm impressed. How did you manage it?"

"Catalogues. I never even set foot out of my house this year."

"You're kidding!"

"Nope. From wrapping paper to outdoor lights, I've ordered it all from one catalogue or another."

"Gee, you didn't happen to come across any electric slippers, did you?" I had given up on trying to find them in time for Christmas, and since I had lost the original catalogue in which I had seen them, I couldn't even order them for Helen's birthday.

"No, but you might try L. L. Bean. They deal in a lot of cold-weather merchandise," Maggie suggested. She laughed, adding, "Trust me. I know my catalogues!"

"I guess so!" I answered. "But you mean to tell me you haven't been to a mall all month? Even to visit Santa's Workshop?" I persisted.

"Oh, well, if you want to get technical, yes, I did take the kids over so that Ryan could cry and Amanda could roll her eyes around at how dumb the whole thing was. Megan's the only one who looks forward to going."

"Amanda doesn't believe in Santa anymore?" I asked, more interested in this information than anything L. L. Bean had to offer.

"Oh, gosh, no. She figured that out last year. I even wonder about Megan. She says she does, but not with a lot of conviction. I guess this'll be her last year." Maggie sighed and I guessed she was thinking that no longer believing in Santa Claus marked another passage in time. I knew I was.

"I hate to see it happen, really," I said, voicing my thoughts. "It doesn't seem like they get much of a chance to enjoy it. I mean, they don't really understand much of what's happening until they're three or four, and then by six or seven it's all over!"

"Yeah, I know what you mean," Maggie agreed. "But I'd like to think that there's more to Christmas than believing in Santa Claus. And Amanda adjusted just fine. In some ways I think it takes a little of the pressure off them, if you know what I mean."

I thought back to what Dr. Salk had said about kids realizing that it's people who give the gifts, and I answered, "Oh, Maggie, you're such a good mother!"

"Oh, sure, tell that to my kids." She laughed, but I could tell she was pleased with the compliment. Who wouldn't be? Compliments are few and far between for most mothers. You practically have to go into therapy if you want to hear someone tell you you're doing a good job. "Amy still believes, then?" Maggie asked.

"Well, yes and no. She just asked me today if Santa was real. I avoided a direct answer."

"I'd tell her. She's too old and too smart not to figure it out this year, and it'll just be awkward for both of you if you don't," Maggie advised.

"You're probably right," I answered.

"Oh! There's my doorbell!" Maggie cried. "It's probably the UPS man."

We quickly made plans to get together after Christmas before she rushed off to sign for the day's delivery.

What My Mother Said

Needless to say, my mother was opposed to the whole thing. "Don't you *dare* tell her Santa isn't real! It'll ruin her Christmas!" she insisted over the phone later that same day.

"Mom, she's eight years old. *Nobody* believes in Santa Claus in the third grade," I defended my position.

"Well, I hate to tell you what grade I was in before I found out the truth . . . fifth."

"Oh, my God, Mother. And didn't you feel like a fool? Weren't you the least bit annoyed with your parents for allowing you to believe for so long?" I asked.

"Well, of course I felt like a fool, who wouldn't? But I was terribly disappointed, too. It spoiled my whole Christmas, and it'll spoil Amy's, too. And what about Katie-who-never-misses-a-trick? Amy'll make a slip and she'll have it figured out in a flash."

"Oh, I don't think so. Kids turn a deaf ear to stuff they don't want to know about. If Katie wants to believe in Santa Claus, she'll rationalize any so-called "slips" Amy may make. Come on, Mom, this is *Katie* we're talking about!"

"Well, I suppose. But I still think you're wrong. I mean what's the point? Why the big push to make her grow up and 'face reality,' as Jerry would say?"

"Because she *asked,* Mom. She came right out and asked me if Santa was real. I've got to say *something,*" I explained.

"So what's wrong with lying? I did it for you," she reminded me, and suddenly I was six years old again, standing unobserved in the living room doorway as my parents stuffed stockings on Christmas Eve. That was how I had learned the truth about Santa. Overexcited and unable to sleep, I had crept downstairs to see if Santa had come. He had . . . or rather, they had. My mother had explained that Santa was in such a hurry that he had asked them to finish stuffing the stockings. I had gone along with it even though I knew better. In one of those lucid moments that children often have about adults, I realized that it was more important to them that I believe than it was to me.

"I know you did," I answered, returning to our conversation, "but you didn't have to."

"Maybe not, but I remembered how devastated I had been—"

"You were ten years old," I interrupted. "And probably more devastated about being lied to for so long than you were that Santa wasn't real."

"That's possible," she agreed reluctantly. "Just let me know what you decide so I don't look the fool *again!*"

We both laughed, and I promised to keep her posted.

What My Husband Said

There were only two weeks left before Christmas, and Jerry still hadn't guessed his gift. I felt confident I'd make it all the way to Christmas Eve, which is when we always *say* we'll exchange gifts but we never do because he's always guessed his by then. But he's not one to give up easily.

"Is it something I said I wanted within the last six weeks?" Jerry asked that evening while I cut up vegetables for the salad.

"I'm not answering any of your questions," I said. "And anyway, I have something more important to discuss with you."

"Let's see, it's not clothes, it's not something for school. . . ." Ignoring my remark, Jerry began reeling off what he had previously deduced about his gift. "Is it something for my truck?" he asked slowly, a light bulb going on inside his head.

Feeling my face go crimson, I turned my back to him and tried as best I could to answer in a noncommittal way, "No, it's not something for your truck. Now stop pestering me and tell me what I should do about Amy and Santa Claus."

Temporarily thrown off guard by my last remark, Jerry asked, "What about Amy and Santa Claus? Has she been seeing that no-good scum behind my back again?" he teased.

"Oh, will you be serious!" I laughed, relieved to have an excuse for the goofy smile I always got when he came close to guessing one of his presents. "Amy asked me today if Santa was real," I explained.

"Well, it's about time. And you told her the truth, I hope," he said in that tone of voice that meant, "You should have, but I bet you didn't."

"I didn't tell her anything one way or the other," I said, falling into his trap. "She caught me off guard . . . and Katie was sitting right there," I continued in my own defense.

"Julie, if *we* don't tell her, then she'll learn about it at school the same way she learned about the facts of life—in line to play handball, from Mike Wilson."

"Oh, please—"

"And think how embarrassed she'll be," he continued. "And how much she'll wish she'd heard it first from you."

I was silent for a moment, thinking about my mother in the fifth grade and me standing in the hallway on Christmas Eve. Now it was Amy's turn and I owed it to her to do it right. Jerry suddenly clapped his hands together, startling me out of my reverie.

"I've got it!" he cried. "Seat covers! You got me seat covers for Christmas!"

"Oh, for heaven's sake, Jerry, I didn't even know you wanted seat covers for that dumb truck," I answered smoothly. But he caught sight of my foolish grin, and before I could do any more denying, he dashed off to search for his present.

I heard him call to me from the deep recesses of the closet, "You may as well let me have them early since I already know what it is!"

188 ♦ What's a Mom to Do!

What I Did

That night as I tucked Amy into bed I said, "You asked me earlier today if Santa was real or not. Why?"

"Because I wanted to know."

"Really?" I asked quietly pulling the old "reverse parry."

"Really." And our eyes met.

"No, Amy he's not a real living man. It's a myth, an old, old story, told all around the world to make Christmas more fun for children. But by your age most kids figure it out and just enjoy pretending about Santa." This came to me spontaneously, but I liked it because it didn't sound as if she had to give him up altogether.

"I thought so," Amy answered after a thoughtful silence.

"I'm sorry if I've disappointed you," I whispered, my throat tightening on every word.

"Well, it sure answers a lot of questions, anyway. At least now I won't lie awake wondering about apartments without chimneys, lists that get lost, or how old Santa is. It's kind of a relief, really."

"Oh, Amy, I love you!" I laughed, hugging her close.

She chuckled and said, "Hey, does this mean I don't have to worry about being good or bad?"

"Are you kidding?" I answered. "Now you've got Santa Claus living right under your own roof!"

"Oh, no!" Amy rolled her eyes in dismay.

Giving her one last hug, I asked, "Are you okay?"

"Yeah, but I think I'm going to miss the excitement."

"Oh, honey, Christmas is filled with excitement that Santa was only a part of. You'll see. And we'll still pretend about Santa, for Katie, you know."

"Oh, that's right. She doesn't know, does she?"

"No, she has a couple more years until she's old enough to understand like you do."

I thought that'd do the trick, and I was pleased when she answered, "Yeah, she's too little to handle it."

I left her then, alone with her thoughts, and even though she said she was fine it was a long time before she finally fell asleep.

So what about the red flannel nightgowns—is that what you want to know? Well, I never did get around to making them, which was just as well because the material came in very handy several months later for Superman capes.

And because of Amy's rather traumatic experience I did make a speed run back to the mall for a Kimberly Cheerleader doll. And, in the perpetual struggle to keep things even, I got Katie a My Little Pony Stable (not only of pink plastic but with many moving parts that definitely required assembly).

The Moroccan candlesticks didn't turn out half bad, making presentable gifts to understanding grandparents (blinded by love is what we were counting on), and in order to incorporate the pink flash cubes and gold six-pack holders, we bought Amy and Katie their very own tree for the playroom. The perforated tin cans I kept for the downstairs tree because once they were fitted with white bulbs they looked quite lovely in conjunction with my wonderland setup from last year.

All in all it was a wonderful Christmas. Amy was, indeed, "wise enough to recognize the Santa Claus story for what it was," and after the initial shock wore off, she discovered Christmas to be as exciting as ever.

Silent night, holy night . . .

10

The Issue
of Illness

Amy burst into the room, flung herself down on the couch gasping for air and cried out, "Oh! Mommy! My tummy!" I offered her a drink of water and told her to go to the bathroom. I'd been through this before. The first time she had doubled over in apparent agony, moaning, "Oh, oh! My tummy hurts *so bad!*" I had been alarmed and wondered what "hurts so bad" could possibly be symptomatic of. The flu, or just gas? Appendicitis, or just a side-ache? I asked where it hurt, when it hurt, and how it hurt, but before I could figure out *why* it hurt, she had leaped up, spun around twice and announced, "It's gone! I feel great!" and dashed off. And since then I had learned to ignore her outbursts. Stomach ailments didn't threaten me. I mean if it *is* the flu she'll throw up or something, and if it's appendicitis she just won't leap up and dash off again. But my lack of sympathy annoys her no end, and she stubbornly lies on the couch making low, groaning sounds until the spasm passes, at which time she walks haughtily out of the room. Her parting words—"Well, I guess I'm okay now . . . not that anyone cares!"—are usually accompanied by an icy look of indignation.

Yes, I've learned how to handle legs that itch (try hand lotion), bottoms that tickle (check for carpet fuzz), and feet that tingle (walk it off). And while exterior wounds may be frightening, at least you know where you stand. It's the earache that I dread. This is bad news because an aching ear could mean infection, which, in turn, not only means a trip to the doctor and costly medicine, but, if not treated in time, a sleepless night. Then again, it could be nothing more than a passing twinge. But to be on the safe side I try to determine the severity of an earache as soon as possible.

The last time I faced this dilemma it was Sunday evening around six-thirty (kids only get sick at night and on weekends, you know). Out of the corner of my eye I saw Amy slapping at the side of her head.

"What are you doing?"

"My ear is all plugged up."

"Oh." I knew better than to let my anxiety show—they feed on it, you know. So I casually answered, "Well, some cough syrup ought to take care of that." Having been through this before, I knew that cough syrup sometimes helps drain plugged ears, which just might avert an infection (aren't you impressed?).

"No, I hate that stuff! It hardens in my throat!"

"What?"

"It does! It hardens and I can't breathe."

"That's nonsense. It just soothes your throat if you've been coughing a lot."

"Well, I don't have a cough, and anyway my ear feels fine now."

"Oh? It isn't plugged?"

"Not really."

"Not really? What do you mean? Does it hurt?"

"Just so-so."

" 'So-so, not really'! Honestly, Amy, make up your mind! Does your ear hurt or not?" We were approaching the point of no return. It's bad enough to call a doctor at eight o'clock on Sunday evening, especially if it turns out to be nothing, but any time later than that is really out of the question. So unless it's a real emergency, the kind with heavy blood loss or temperatures that shoot up to 104 degrees, we pretty much stick it out until office hours the next morning. With less than an hour to go before my eight-o'clock deadline, I watched Amy carefully throughout dinner. Her body twitched periodically, and every now and then a grimace would pass across her face. Once she let out a startled "Oh!" and looked at me expectantly. I ignored it. No eye contact, remember. But as I put her to bed, gasping for air because of the treacherous cough syrup, I had the sinking feeling I hadn't seen the last of her for the evening.

And sure enough, I was rousted out of bed at ten, again at one, and a third time at four by her cries of "Mommy! Mommy! Come here!" I gave her some baby aspirin the first time around, elevated her head with an extra pillow the second time, and told her she was overreacting the third. In an attempt to determine whether her hysterics were warranted, I asked, "Does it really hurt *that* badly?"

And she answered, "Kind of." At four A.M. I want to hear "kind of"? So we got into "On a scale of one to ten . . ." and "Compared to the time you slammed your finger in the car door . . ." and in the end I gave her some more aspirin and the hot-water bottle. The next day Dr. Williams verified Amy's story. The left ear was definitely infected. Vindicated, Amy spent the rest of the day on the couch, pale and helpless, with a quilt pulled up over her, watching TV. Every now and then she'd call weakly for me to change the channel or bring her some more ginger ale. Yes, humbled by the fact that she really was sick, I'd made a speed run to the market for the standard sick bay supplies; Jell-o, chicken noodle soup, orange sherbet, chewable aspirin, and a new coloring book. Actually, I don't mind this stage of illness. With the house warm and cozy, I make phone calls in a quiet voice to cancel my hair appointment and rearrange car pools. It's nice to be needed again, since most of the time all I hear is, "Mom, I can do it myself!" It isn't this day of indulgence that bothers me. No, it's the days or even hours prior to it, when they're deciding just how sick they are, that drives me nuts.

I looked up from the bills scattered across the kitchen table, to where Amy was lying on the couch staring moodily at the ceiling.

"Do you want an apple?" I asked pleasantly, figuring this was one of those hunger-pain stomachaches.

"No, it'll just hurt to eat it," she answered dramatically.

"Your stomach hurts *that* badly?" I questioned her sharply. Her refusal of food set off a first-stage sick alert in the back of my mind.

"No, my throat. It'll hurt my throat," she answered.

"I thought you said your tummy hurt." I said, beginning to feel annoyed. How come they never know precisely what part of them hurts? How come they always say they have a headache just before they throw up all over your shoes?

"Well, now it's my throat," Amy answered, and seeing that she had my attention, she clenched her teeth as she raised a small hand to her neck.

I automatically checked my watch: 4:45. But at least it was only Thursday. Still, I didn't like the sound of it, and I watched her closely for the next few minutes. Amy and Katie *never* got sore throats, and I didn't like being on unfamiliar ground.

"Are you sure it's not your stomach?" I asked hopefully.

"It's both," she answered. I had set myself up for that one. Deciding upon preventive medicine, I offered Amy some children's aspirin and a glass of water.

"Just in case," I said, standing beside the couch. After chewing up the tablets and taking a few sips of water, she decided to go back to the handball game in progress on our garage door. I breathed a sigh of relief and began fixing dinner.

I didn't hear about Amy's throat again until the next morning.

"It hurts to swallow," she announced, twisting up her face in that way people do when they try to swallow with a sore throat.

"Oh, you probably slept with your mouth open last night and now your throat's just a little dry," I assured her. I'm a firm believer in positive thinking. Over 90 percent of what ails people is psychosomatic, you know (well, some percentage anyway).

Amy looked at me skeptically and repeated, "It hurts," and again she scrunched her face into a series of contortions.

"Don't do that, Amy," I said. I was trying very hard to make the whole thing go away.

"What?" she asked innocently.

"Make faces at the table." Since I was irritated by this lingering sore throat yet unwilling to acknowledge the possibility of its legitimacy, Amy's face became the target of my annoyance.

"I can't help it. It's the only way I can drink my juice," Amy said a little too pathetically to be convincing.

"Then eat your cereal," I answered, still ignoring the issue.

I glanced up at the clock, seven-thirty. School started at

eight-thirty. Was she too sick to go? I snuck a glance in her direction. She was shoveling oatmeal into her mouth. Oh, she's fine, I thought to myself. But then, as she attempted to swallow her face became gripped in the familiar distortion. Darn!

"Mommy," Katie called. "Amy's making faces again."

"Just ignore her," I advised Katie. Goodness knows, *I* am!

Then, feeling a pang of guilt, I said to Amy, "Let me *see* your throat." The time had come for some action. Put up or shut up, as they say. Amy yawned big and wide, but her tongue wouldn't flatten down so I could see. Picking up a spoon, I pressed the back of the handle against her tongue to get a better view.

"Gosh, you have a fat tongue," I commented. "But other than that you look okay." Her throat did look a little red, and what I thought were spots of pus turned out to be bits of oatmeal, but I didn't tell *her* all that. "Let me see *your* throat, Katie." Without anything to compare it to, I really couldn't tell whether Amy's throat was abnormal or not. I had used this comparison technique once before when I had noticed a swelling of the lymph nodes along Amy's groin. She was doing back bends in a leotard, and these small lumps came to my attention. Actually I didn't know they were lymph nodes until I looked it up in *The Parents' Encyclopedia*. There I found a diagram of the various locations of these "glands" and the warning that lymph node swelling in children should be examined by the doctor because, "while the vast majority of cases will be a local infection, such swelling could be symptomatic of leukemia or Hodgkin's disease." There it was, every mother's nightmare. But just to be sure I wasn't imagining things, I had Amy lie flat on her back so I could examine her. Yes, there they were, small little mounds of tissue like you find under your neck when you have a cold. Instinctively I felt Katie's lymph nodes as well. Oh, my God! Hers were swollen too! What could this mean? Infectious leukemia? Had the girls been introduced to some new strain of contagious cancer? Quick as a flash I flattened myself out on the floor and reached down to feel my own glands. I knew what I would find and I was right. Oh, no! I remember thinking, we're all going to die! Struggling for composure, I had called our family doctor, who assured me that the slight swelling of these "glands" was nothing to be alarmed about. Like the glands under the jaw, these had become enlarged due to a recent rash of colds. I hung up the phone with a new lease on life. This episode flashed through my mind in the split second before I looked at Katie's throat.

Opening wide, Katie was happy to be examined. I peered into her mouth. "Holy cow!" I cried out in alarm.

"What?" both children asked in unison. Katie snapped her mouth shut, suddenly regretting having volunteered for inspection.

"Your tonsils are *huge,*" I answered. "Let me see again." She shook her head, but I assuaged her doubts by adding, "It's okay, honey. I think this explains your snoring."

"I don't snore," she insisted. Why do they always say that? Katie allowed me a second look, and even Amy got to take a peek, although I don't think she knew what she was looking for. But as large as her tonsils were, they didn't appear to be infected. And Amy's throat was decidedly redder.

"Let me take your temperature," I said to Amy. I needed further data. Amy sat at the kitchen table rattling the thermometer around in her mouth.

"Hold it under your tongue," I reminded her, "or I'll have to use your other end." Under the threat of a rectal reading Amy clamped her mouth closed over the thermometer. A few minutes later I removed the instrument and studied it carefully. Hmm, I wouldn't consider 99.8 a *temperature,* really, would you? I stared at Amy long and hard, trying to decide whether or not to send her to school.

The last time I had to make this decision Amy had been up half the night with an earache. But around one-thirty she had fallen into a deep sleep and didn't awaken until seven-thirty. I had taken that as a good sign and packed her a lunch for school.

"You're not sending her to school, are you?" Jerry had asked incredulously.

"Well," I answered defensively, "I won't be able to get her in to the doctor until after one o'clock anyway, and being at school will keep her mind off it. I'll have to get someone to cover for me at work as it is."

Just then Amy had staggered into the kitchen clutching the side of her head.

"So, Amy, what do you think? Feel well enough to go to school today?" She and her father had exchanged looks of total disbelief. But she felt better after having some breakfast, and by eight-fifteen she was dressed and ready to go.

At nine-thirty the school called me at work. Amy was in the nurse's office with a *severe* earache, they told me accusingly. I took off from work, slunk into the office, and hustled Amy out, making eye contact with no one.

Not wanting to go through *that* again, I said, "Amy, I'm thinking of keeping you home today. Because of your throat."

"No!" Amy protested adamantly. "We're going to finish our coil pottery today, and Jessica promised me she'd bring her sticker collection to school."

"Oh. Then you feel well enough to go?"

"Oh, sure," she answered, but not with as much enthusiasm as I'd have like her to. "I just won't swallow."

"Oh, Amy, if it's *that* bad . . ."

"I'm just kidding, Mom," she laughed. "I'll be fine."

"Well, okay," I answered uncertainly. I probably should have asked her in the first place.

After she left for school, though, I began to have second thoughts. What if she had strep throat? What if it was tonsillitis? She had a birthday party to attend Saturday, and Sunday was our church picnic. I decided to do a little research. After all, it *was* Friday, and if I wanted to make a doctor's appointment I'd have to act fast.

What the Books Said

"A sore throat should not be taken lightly and just treated with aspirin, gargles ot throat lozenges," said the authors of *The Parents' Encyclopedia*. "At times the side effects may be much worse than the sore throat itself. Scarlet fever and the dangerous diseases rheumatic fever and acute nephritis are caused by streptococcus sore throats. . . . It is therefore important that a doctor's advice be sought in every case of a sore throat in children." I want you to keep in mind that this is the same book that had me believing we were all dying of leukemia. Now it was scarlet fever. Can't a person just have a simple cold anymore? As if in answer to my question, the author, Dr. Levine, continued to explain in his "Signs and Symptoms" section that a sore throat could be caused by either a bacterial infection or a virus, as in the common cold. The throat is usually fiery red, and white patches may appear on the tonsils in the case of a bacterial infection, but those due to viruses leave the throat only slightly red. I had checked for white patches, remember? They had turned out to be oatmeal. As far as treatment went, Dr. Levine explained that while infections caused by a bacteria could be treated with an antibiotic, viruses did not respond to such medication but usually cleared up in a few days. More than likely, Amy's was a simple virus—but how to know for sure?

There were four different kinds of sore throats in Dr. Spock's *Baby and Child Care:* in diphtheria, in pharyngitis, in scarlet fever, and in tonsillitis. Gee, there was that scarlet fever again! I turned to page 501, deciding to check it out. "Scarlet fever usually begins with some of these symptoms: sore throat [gulp], vomiting, fever, headache. The rash is not apt to appear for a day or two." Oh, it has a rash. At least I now knew what to look for. "With tonsillitis," I read, "the child usually has a high fever . . . headache . . . vomiting . . . tonsils become fiery read and swollen . . . white patches. . . ." Well, Amy didn't have a fever (remember, we agreed it was not worth mentioning), and her throat certainly wasn't what you'd consider "fiery red." Dr Spock concluded his "Other Throat Infections" section by saying, "The doctor should be called if there is any fever [any?] or if the child looks sick [what child doesn't?] or if the throat is more than slightly sore (even if there is no fever)." What I want to know is, how does one determine "more than slightly sore"? Isn't this just a fancy way of saying "kind of"? I had a lot of trouble with "kind of," if I remember correctly, and had no intention of tackling "more than slightly sore."

In more need of common sense than I was of medical jargon, I looked up "Illness" in *The Mother's Almanac*—or "Health Care," as they call it. From bites, burns, and bumps to sprains, stings, and stomachaches, they had something useful to say. I learned how to give an appendicitis test by slowly poking the abdomen with stiff fingers (if it hurts more when you push them *in,* it's probably gas, but if it hurts more when you pull them *out,* it may be appendicitis) and to serve a child apple juice, gelatin, and cottage cheese for diarrhea or whole wheat along with two tablespoons of prune juice for constipation. And after the difficulty I had this morning keeping Amy's mouth shut while taking her temperature, I found the suggestion to let a child "listen to Weather, Dial-a-Prayer or any other thing that will talk nonstop" quite clever, not to mention a good distraction from the indignity of a rectal reading. For a sore throat the authors recommended a gargle made up of three ounces of boiled water, one tablespoon of hydrogen peroxide, and a quarter teaspoon of salt. "The disadvantage is the taste," warns Ms. Kelly, "but the results are worth it." They also recommend that if a fever develops to call a doctor. The fever seemed to be an important factor. That and small white patches on the tonsils. But there wasn't much I could do until Amy either got home from school or they called for me to come pick her up—whichever came first.

What Maggie Said

Katie's ride to preschool had come and gone, and although I was *supposed* to spend the next two and a half (precious) hours making phone calls for the school jog-athon, I decided to give Maggie a call first.

"Julie! I was just going to call *you!*" Maggie said in a surprised voice.

"Oh?"

"Yes," and then she explained, "I was hoping we could get together this weekend. Tom's out of town and I was looking for things to fill the time with."

"Oh, thanks," I teased. "So now I'm just filler, huh?"

"Oh, you know what I mean." Maggie laughed.

"Yeah, I *do* know what you mean. Weekends tend to drag when he's out of town, right?"

"Exactly. I just thought if you guys weren't busy . . ." Maggie trailed off.

"Not at all," I answered cheerfully, trying to remember what *time* that birthday party was and just *how long* the picnic would last.

"Well, great!" Maggie sounded relieved, and I was glad I hadn't mentioned the other commitments. We could work it out.

"The only problem I can see," I warned her, "is if Amy's sick. She's been complaining of a sore throat, and I almost kept her home from school today."

"Really? Megan had strep throat last month and I didn't even know it until I took her to the dentist, and after looking down her throat *he* told me to call her doctor. I was so embarrassed. Good for the image, right?"

"Didn't she complain about it hurting?" I asked.

"Not really, she said her *jaw* hurt, and so I figured she was getting in her molars," Maggie explained. See? Kids are all the same.

"Typical," I commented.

"Anyway, if she runs a fever you should take her in," Maggie advised. This seemed to be the general consensus. "Otherwise, check for molars!" Maggie laughed and then added, "Freeze a few cups of juice and let her chip away at them if her throat still bothers her. The ice will numb the pain a little, and if she does have a fever it'll stop her from becoming dehydrated."

"You're too much, Maggie," I said good-naturedly. "All those magazine subscriptions are finally paying off. Only in *Redbook* would you find information like that."

"Family Circle," Maggie corrected me. "And I've got a whole stack of them to pass along!"

"Well, bring them with you this weekend. I'll call you later and let you know how Amy's feeling and we'll set something up."

"Great! I'll talk to you later."

We hung up, and I quickly poured some orange juice into a large plastic cup and stuck it in the freezer before I forgot.

What My Mother Said

My mother caught me between phone calls about an hour later.

"How would it be if I picked Amy up from school today? I promised her she could help me pot plants this afternoon."

"Well . . ." I hesitated.

Misunderstanding my reluctance, she added, "Katie can come, too, of course."

"Oh, it's not that," I assured her. "Amy's got a sore throat. I may be taking her to the doctor's this afternoon."

"Oh, dear. Is she home from school, then?"

"No," I answered, a little embarrassed. "She said she felt well enough to go. . . . I took her temperature," I added weakly.

"Oh, I'm sure she's fine. School will keep her mind off it," she answered matter-of-factly. So *that's* where I got that theory—I inherited it.

"Anyway, if she doesn't feel better this afternoon, or if she's running a fever, I'll take her in. It could be strep throat or tonsillitis," I said with a note of authority. (No point in mentioning scarlet fever, though.)

"I'll bet she's just coming down with a cold," my mother answered. "She's been awfully busy lately. Give her a few days of peace and quiet with plenty of rest and she'll be fine." It was my mother's answer to everything—and it usually worked.

"Well, just to be on the safe side I might take her in. It's Friday and I hate to go through the weekend worrying."

"You're right. And let's pass on potting plants until next week."

Hanging up the phone, I considered my mother's advice of peace, quiet, and rest. Sure, we'll have a little peace just before the birthday party, plan on quiet after the picnic, and work in some rest around our visit with Maggie.

What My Husband Said

I could hardly believe my eyes when Jerry burst into the kitchen at two-fifteen.

"What are *you* doing home?" I asked. "Are you sick?" Since I had half expected to have Amy home early, I just assumed the worst when Jerry walked through the door three hours earlier than usual (and is there anything worse than a sick husband?).

"No, no," he said hurriedly as I followed him into the bedroom. "There's a meeting down at the district office in fifteen minutes and I've got to change my pants," he indicated a big tear down the side of his pants.

"How did you do that?"

"Oh, I got caught on some sort of hook while trying to maneuver the film projector out of the equipment room." He was already stepping into some fresh slacks. "It's been a bad day all around, and now I've got to go convince the assistant superintendant that we need a drug intervention program. . . ." He paused before adding, "You can't expect people to take you seriously when your pants are flapping in the breeze." I laughed and was reminded of how like him Amy was. They were never at a loss for words.

"Well, good luck. If we're not home when you get back, we're probably at the doctor's office," I explained.

"Oh? Who's sick?"

"I think Amy. You know how her throat has been bothering her? Well, I thought I'd have Dr. Williams look at it before we got into the weekend."

"Good thinking," he answered, heading back toward the kitchen.

"So you think I should?" I asked, trailing behind him. I knew he was preoccupied and I felt stupid even bringing it up, but, bustling around the house, gathering up important data for his meeting, he radiated confidence, and in my weakened state of insecurity I hoped he'd throw some in my direction.

"What?"

"Take her to the doctor's . . . Amy . . ." I repeated.

"Oh, well, if that's what you think you should do. You know more about this than I do."

"I do?"

"Sure! I have complete faith in you," he said, grabbing an apple as he passed through the kitchen. "See you at dinner," he called, closing the door with a bang.

Complete faith, huh? Well, if I was going to live up to his expectations, I'd better get going.

What I Did

Amy walked through the door only minutes later.

"Hi, honey! How are you feeling?" I asked anxiously.

"Okay, but my throat still hurts," she answered. I offered her a glass of apple juice and a handful of pretzels and sat across from her at the kitchen table, studying her pale face. Dark circles were beginning to develop beneath her eyes.

She drank her juice and then, looking at the pretzels, said, "I don't feel like anything else."

I reached across the table and rested my hand on her forehead. It felt warm. "I want to take your temperature again," I said, leaving the room to retrieve the thermometer. Shaking it down, I thought about what I had read in *The Mother's Almanac*. "Do you want to listen to Dial-a-Story while you're having your temperature taken?"

"Yeah!" Amy answered, delighted with the idea. I dialed the number printed on an elephant bookmark that Amy had brought home from the public library last week. She sat quietly, chuckling now and then, for a full four minutes before announcing, "It's over."

"Was it a good story?" I asked, taking the thermometer from her mouth.

"Uh-huh . . ." And as she proceeded to give me a blow-by-blow account of "The City Mouse and the Country Mouse," I studied the line of mercury that had climbed to a substantial 101.5 degrees.

"I knew it," I sighed, and reaching for the phone, I dialed the number of our family doctor.

It was two forty-five and the receptionist wasn't sure that she could fit Amy in. "Today?" she said incredulously. But when I mentioned the possibility of scarlet fever, she decided the doctor could squeeze us in at four-thirty.

Having proof of her illness only made Amy feel that much worse, and as she lay on the couch whimpering softly, I remembered the cup of frozen juice in the freezer. For the next hour and a half she chipped happily away, listening to a tape of *Annie*. Pleased with my control of the situation, I actually felt deserving of Jerry's "complete faith." Thank goodness Maggie reads *Family Circle*!

"My throat feels much better," Amy commented on our way to her four-thirty appointment.

"Really?" I said noncommitally. Why do they always feel better in the car? She chatted happily with her sister and even sang us a song she'd learned at school that day.

But sitting on the paper-covered bed in the examining room, Amy looked small and vulnerable. She answered the doctor's questions in a soft voice and only managed a smile when it came time to choose something from the toy box. While Dr. Williams ruled out tonsillitis, he did think she could have contracted streptococcus. He took a throat culture that would be ready Monday and gave me a prescription for penicillin for the meantime.

"Keep her quiet and give her plenty of liquids," he advised, patting Amy affectionately on the head.

Before leaving, I asked him to take a quick peek at Katie's tonsils. He agreed that they were enlarged, but said they looked healthy and that unless she complained of a sore throat to ignore them. And, yes, it did explain the snoring.

On the way home we stopped to have Amy's prescription filled and to pick up a few things from the market: rainbow sherbet, alphabet soup . . . and oh, there was this great book of 101 paper tricks. . . .

I know what you're thinking, and, no, Amy did not attend the Saturday birthday party. She played quietly most of the day and even took a nap—a sure sign, my mother commented later, that she had been overtired. And instead of getting together with the kids, Maggie got a baby-sitter and she and I went to dinner and the movies Saturday night, something we decided we should do more often!

We all stayed home from the church picnic Sunday. Using Amy's throat as our excuse, we spent a peaceful day doing nothing, something else we decided should be done more often.

Epilogue

So, what do you think? Am I on the right track? Would I make Mrs. Piggle-Wiggle proud? Of course I can't take all the credit (blame?). I had help. And just in case you didn't get the message, help is what this book is all about. Parenting isn't something we can, or even should, do alone. It's a job too tough and too important to tackle singlehanded. So, the next time your six-year-old has no socks to wear because they all have funny nubs on them or your three-year-old won't go to sleep at night until a bedtime ritual of stories, songs, kisses and hugs has been completed, talk about it, check it out. You're not alone! You share with struggling parents everywhere the responsibility and challenge of a lifetime. And the only thing that keeps us going is a love for our children like no other love on this earth. And this we share, too.

I also want to remind you that what you have just read is a true story. Sure, a few names and places have been changed to protect the innocent, but basically I've tried to stick as close to the truth as possible. I only bring this up because of my editor's concern that too many of the chapters featured Amy while only a few were exclusively Katie's. "But she's the oldest," I had explained. "The readers will understand." And you do, don't you? I resisted the suggestion to change things around so that Katie appeared more often. "It won't be realistic," I had argued. "The readers will see that."And you would have, wouldn't you? After all, Katie was only five years old at the close of *What's a Mom to Do?*—just coming into her own, really. Not that I anticipate any problems in the immediate future, mind you. What could go wrong in kindergarten? How hard could memorizing 105 sight words be? No, I have a handle on this now. I wasn't tricked into Halloween Carnival Chairman, I volunteered. I know what I'm doing. And third grade? A piece of cake. How long could it possibly take for Amy to learn her times tables? . . . Are you thinking what I'm thinking? You may not have heard the last of us yet!